A CHILD IN BERLIN

*The Poignant Story of
Heidi Posnien and Her Mother
During the Fall of Germany*

RHONDA LAURITZEN

A POST HILL PRESS BOOK
ISBN: 979-8-88845-908-9
ISBN (eBook): 979-8-88845-909-6

A Child in Berlin:
The Poignant Story of Heidi Posnien and Her Mother During the Fall of Germany
© 2024 by Rhonda Lauritzen
All Rights Reserved

Cover design by Cody Corcoran

This book, as well as any other Post Hill Press publications, may be purchased in bulk quantities at a special discounted rate. Contact orders@posthillpress.com for more information.

All people, locations, events, and situations are portrayed to the best of the author's memory. While all of the events described are true, many names and identifying details have been changed to protect the privacy of the people involved.

No part of this book may be reproduced, stored in a retrieval system, or transmitted by any means without the written permission of the author and publisher.

Post Hill Press
New York • Nashville
posthillpress.com

Published in the United States of America
1 2 3 4 5 6 7 8 9 10

From Heidi to Käthe and Oma:
Everything I am, I am because of the two of you.
Also, to my children and grandchildren.
May you know the courage and light that you have inherited.

TABLE OF CONTENTS

Author's Note 7
Preface—July 2019 9

Chapter One — January 1939 13
Chapter Two — August to September 1, 1939 33
Chapter Three — September 1, 1939 to December, 1940 ... 42
Chapter Four — January 1941 through mid-1941 59
Chapter Five — Mid-1941 through December 1941 76
Chapter Six — January 1942 through mid-1942 94
Chapter Seven — Mid-1942 through December 1942 ... 102
Chapter Eight — 1943 129
Chapter Nine — 1944 143
Chapter Ten — January through March 1945 163
Chapter Eleven — April through December 1945 184
Chapter Twelve — 1946 through 1949 205

Epilogue 230
Bibliography 233
Review Inquiry 237
About the Author 238

AUTHOR'S NOTE

WE HAVE ATTEMPTED TO ACCURATELY portray the characters, events, and historical setting of this story, which was written from Heidi's perspective as gleaned from her oral history. These recollections were aided by extensive research and overlaid onto the historical timeline.

Most of the large and small details are described as Heidi remembered them. Her memories were remarkably vivid and withstood external verification. Thus, no people, circumstances, or scenes were invented from whole cloth, and we exercised restraint when tempted to overstep parts relating to the adults in Heidi's life where she was not privy to the details. We wish we knew more about aspects of the story relating to the life of Heidi's mother, Käthe, but she is not here to ask. Dialogue has been recreated, and readers can assume that some liberties were taken to reconstruct scenes involving Käthe where Heidi was not physically present. However, we often left gaps rather than invent fiction.

Footnotes throughout the narrative paint a broader picture of historical context. These mostly relate to matters which young Heidi could not have known at the time. A few indicate where there were unknowns in the factual record.

A question that some American readers have asked is how to pronounce Käthe's name. In German it is produced, "Kate-uh." If it is easier, you can call her the English equivalent, "Kate."

One character bears particular acknowledgment. We decided not to embellish details about Lizzie's boyfriend, instead limiting our descriptions to what Heidi saw and heard for herself. Our intent was to be respectful and not invent him. We do not even know his name, let alone his full story. Thus, rather than creating a fictitious character, we intentionally left his life as a gaping hole in the story. His life serves as a reminder of but one human tragedy among the six million Jews and the other groups who were murdered. That is a saga we felt woefully unqualified to do justice.

We also acknowledge the inherent unfairness that most of the people we have written about are deceased and cannot correct our understanding if we got something wrong. This story is Heidi's truth, and we apologize in advance for any missteps.

PREFACE

JULY 2019

It's a bluebird July morning and I draw in the green smell of mowed pasture. Across from me sits one of the classiest women I have ever met. Heidi Posnien has the sort of peaceful confidence that makes people feel comfortable. She was a clothing model for thirty years and is still a strikingly beautiful woman.

I remember how, at first, I could hardly hear a German accent in her voice, but now I notice it comes out stronger when we delve into the past. She'll often land on a German or French word first and then will try to translate it across cultures. She only learned a little Polish because even Oma (grandma) spoke German to her, and recently she mused about how she's starting to dream in German again as we work on the Berlin years of her story.

Today, we're seated in wicker chairs looking across the acreage where Heidi and her husband once bred racehorses, peacocks, and St. Bernard dogs. Next to the idyllic turn-of-the-century barn sits an enclosure where Heidi's pet bobcat had lived when he wasn't roaming the house. Behind Heidi, there's a window from which she served hot chocolate and chili when they gathered for ice skating parties on the flooded, frozen pasture. And on summer days like this, her family would descend wooden steps onto the lakeshore to motorboat with friends.

She still has a quick wit and rich memory, so I always have a digital recorder running. Our collaboration has been a rich one, combining her stories with my love of helping it take shape on the page. She is not a confident reader because by the time schools in Berlin picked up after the war, she'd already missed whole swaths of education. Then, when she came to America, she had to start over and learn English—her fourth language. Later, she'd discover the word *dyslexia*, which explained why such a bright girl could have trouble in school.

Ours is a weekly ritual, and each time, she enriches my understanding with new details.

"Wait, you're just now telling me that your mother went to a dinner hosted by *Hitler* himself?" She enjoys the element of surprise, allowing me to discover the story for myself, one clue at a time. Then she dishes out details.

"Yes, that's when she was an opera singer dating a military officer who was assigned to the personal staff for Magda Goebbels, the propaganda minister's wife. My mother never had anything to do with the Nazi party, and this boyfriend even stole a shortwave radio from his employer and gave it to my mother. When he was invited to a formal dinner, at the Reichstag, my mother was arm candy. Adolf Hitler himself sat at the head of the table. That was before people had wised up to Hitler."

Today Heidi and I have photos and letters before us. She picks up a framed group picture and says, "Everyone here is gone now." It's a recurring theme as we thumb through the artifacts of her life. Still, she has an upbeat air about her, and a quick sense of humor. I'm always in a better mood after having spent an afternoon here. Busy as my life is, I never rush our visits, letting the conversation meander through decades, while we also catch up on current events. Next, she hands me a typed letter, and I read it aloud.

My Heidi,

Sixty-five years ago, I found the most beautiful woman I had ever seen, and I wanted to spend every minute of my life with her.

I fell in love with you, Heidi, with a feeling I never had before. After all these years, that feeling has never changed.

My age is taking a toll on me, and next June I will be 87. I can't last much longer, and even though I refused to give up and turn into an old man, I know there must be an end to it. The reason for writing this letter is to tell you that I love you as much now as when we found each other. You were—and are—the love of my life, and you always will be.

I love you.

I wipe a tear that has escaped my eye. It's not the first, nor the last time we will weep together. The writer of that letter is gone now, along with many others.

I ask, "How is it that you're still so happy after so much loss?"

The wisdom that follows comes streaming out in a perfect line, as though they were already queued up and ready for the right moment of release.

"I've told you before that if I'm ever reincarnated, I'd want to be born in America and get an education. Maybe I'd be a fashion designer, or maybe I'd work for the Forest Service. That must come from my father. But I'm grateful for my life. I think about this whole big universe, and I am part of it. I got to be part of it. And I'm me—the parts of my parents and grandparents came together to make me exactly who I am—not anyone else in the world. I get to live this life, and feel, and love. I've been down in the deepest sorrows, but I've also been on the best of highs too. I've eaten this big, beautiful life; I never let it eat me."

This is Heidi's true story as she told it to me one afternoon at a time, over the span of four years. We filled in historical details and some improvisation on the dialogue, but no scenes were invented. We read each draft aloud together. Her memories of the war are strikingly clear.

She says, "When people tell me they don't remember their childhood, I tell them it's because happy childhoods are not that eventful. When you go through something like a war, you remember everything. Even now certain smells and sounds take me right back. I can recall everything about the last days of the war; it was like a whole lifetime."

Hearing her story has been a profound privilege and has inspired me more than I can say, and it has been a tall order to even attempt doing it as well as it deserves. May Heidi's harrowing story bless you with gratitude and may her resilience shine as a beacon for the future.

CHAPTER ONE

JANUARY 1939:
A POLISH FAMILY JUST INSIDE GERMANY

IN THE FOREST OUTSIDE THE village of Mechtal,[1] Heidi clutched her oma's hand with chubby fingers, listening to the sound of snow crunching under their feet.

Grandmother and grandchild followed the same path most evenings to the home of Oma's friend, where several women would gather to gossip while their husbands labored in the coal mine. Miners descended far underground where tunnels spidered out for miles. From the depths, they extracted hard coal, the kind that burned long and hot, and that every country wanted.

Oma carried a sack of feathers harvested from the Christmas goose. That evening, her task would be to remove the stiff quills from each feather to keep them from sticking holes into the bed linings.

Heidi, a precocious child at almost three years old, spent most of her time with Oma while her mother trained in Berlin as an opera singer. Heidi's father never came, so she had had no concept of him.

---

1 The village is a small city called Miechowice in present-day Poland, located near Bytom. After the First World War, the question of whether the area should be granted to Germany or to Poland was put to a vote, and most residents voted to go with Poland. However, the area was a prize because of the coal mines, and Germany ended up getting it despite the vote. Hence, although Heidi's family was ethnically Polish, they were German citizens and spoke both languages perfectly.

Heidi was always glad to go with Oma, but this had been a strange day, with grownups arguing about things she did not understand. Heidi was an only child and the only grandchild, resulting in being around adults only. Without playmates, she spoke clearly for her age and tuned into the grown-up world. However, that day, her family had tried to keep her from knowing what the trouble was.

Now, she pulled free from Oma's hand and lagged to inspect something on the ground. Oma called after her, "Come, child." Heidi scampered to Oma while twirling a wet leaf between her fingers.

The winter forest had already grown dark, so it revealed itself to Heidi through her other senses; she was like a little mouse with her nose twitching as she walked. Indeed, her mother's pet name for the girl was an uncanny fit, "*Mała myszka*," little mouse, and Oma called her "*Mały kociak*," little kitten. Heidi's mother often cooed these words in her native Polish, even though she spoke German to her granddaughter most other times.

This evening, Heidi breathed in the scent of wood smoke from the village, and her ears prickled to hear small mammals scurrying about their work. She imagined larger animals crouching in the night, but she did not fear them. Heidi understood that she and Oma were part of this place, and the old forest was inside them, too.

Heidi pointed at the bright moon casting light upon the snow and said to her grandmother, "*Mein begleiter*," my companion. "He follows me."

Heidi liked the crisp air bracing her cheeks, and she became excited when her nose caught the scent of warm apples roasting. She could smell where they were headed even before spotting a cozy glow filtering through the trees. The home of Oma's friend always felt welcoming.

When Oma and Heidi removed their coats, the women brightened and remarked after the girl. Heidi had dimples and a laugh that made others laugh along with her.

Sometimes the women listened to their German-made Volksempfänger radio, sang songs, gossiped in Polish, and laughed while working together. Then, with busy hands, they commented on news from Germany, which seemed to be itching for a fight with Poland of late.

Their little village and the larger adjacent town of Beuthen (Bytom) had been part of Poland before the Great War, in an area whose boundaries had been redrawn many times through the centuries. The question arose again after the war ended, and it was put up for a vote of the people. Most townsfolk voted to go with Poland, but the coal mines were hotly contested, and their area was ceded to Germany anyway.[2]

Heidi knew nothing of such things, and the rhythm of her life tracked Oma's routines, which felt as ancient as the land.

Tonight, in the firelight, Heidi watched Oma and her friends work on the goose quills. They gave her a roasted apple, and Heidi felt their eyes settle upon her.

The women began clucking about what had happened in Oma's family earlier in the day. The girl fidgeted, understanding that they were talking about her mother and Heidi.

Oma shook her head but then looked toward Heidi with warmth in her eyes and said, "It's no good for a woman to divorce her husband. Käthe should wait it out and keep Heidi with us."

---

[2] The Szyb Zachodni coal mine in Miechowice, Poland (near Bytom) is also known as Western Shaft. It began in 1889 and was fully operational when it opened in 1902. It was owned by Francis Hubert von Tiele-Winckler and was known as the Preussen mine. It was closed in 2005 and most of it was already destroyed.

The day had been a puzzle that Heidi did not understand. The morning began like all the others. Oma got out of bed early so she could attend morning mass at the cathedral as she always did. They lived across from the impressive church with gothic spires and arched stained glass windows. Before leaving, Oma stoked the coal fire awake across from Heidi's fold-up bed in the kitchen.

Heidi's sleepy eyes had opened, and she watched Oma get ready, pulling up her long black hair, holding strands in her mouth while nimble fingers worked it into a tight braid. On weekdays, Oma put on a cotton blouse over a tight layer that secured her large breasts in place. Then she layered no fewer than three cotton skirts and finished with an apron to protect her clothes. She reserved a velvet jacket and her gold taffeta apron with colorful embroidery for Sundays.

Oma was a short but sturdy woman named Veronika Dylong, descended from the Huguenots who fled France under religious persecution in the seventeenth century. Somewhere along the line, they became devout Catholics, and now her married name was Wypych. Her side of the family was more well-off than her husband's, and some gossiped that he married her in hopes of an inheritance. The pair would never see anything of the sort, and they did backbreaking labor to afford an education and music lessons for their children. Käthe was the most musically accomplished of them and played the harmonica, zither, and accordion, but everyone played something. They all sang. Oma and Opa (grandpa) made a comfortable life for their family because they worked in one way or another from morning mass until they lay down in a featherbed of their own making.

After returning from mass that morning, Oma began making the week's rye bread, her arms in the bowl up to her elbows. First, she kneaded it, put it in a covered pan, and stowed it underneath a goose down featherbed. This kept it warm while the dough rose. After a while, she took the pan out, kneaded it again, then put it back under the bedding. When the dough was ready, she shaped it into big round loaves, dusted them with flour, and used a knife to cut the sign of the cross on top. The pans were too big for her kitchen, so she walked them down the street, where the baker's large oven finished them within a few hours.

While the bread baked, Heidi's mother arrived after a two-hour train ride from Berlin.[3] This was a surprise that Heidi had not expected. Neither had Oma.

The days when her mother came home were Heidi's happiest times. Käthe swooped the girl into her arms and smothered her with kisses, getting lipstick all over Heidi's cheeks. They were an affectionate family. Even Oma, who could seem brusque at times, showered the little girl with love.

"My *Schnuckiputzi!*" Sweetie pie, another nickname.

Her mother's name was Katharina Wypych Machinek, but she went by Käthe to German speakers or Kätka to her Polish family. Heidi thought she looked like an angel. Her blonde hair was always done up, and her mother's eyes sparkled like aquamarine gemstones. Käthe was a vibrant twenty-four-year-old and wore modern clothes of the latest city styles, dressing much better than she could afford. This was because she possessed the talent of eyeing a smart outfit in a shop, then the skill to make a pattern out of newspaper and sew a copy at home. She had meticulous attention to detail, matching the best tailors.

Käthe had married Alfred Machinek, a Czech from the countryside whose hometown was an hour away by train. After the scholarship, Käthe couldn't care for her daughter

---

[3] Living inside the German border gave Heidi's family open access to Berlin and other parts of the country.

during the day, so Heidi stayed back in the village. If Oma ever seemed put out by having to watch Heidi, it was an act. Her eldest daughter's talent reflected well on the family, and Heidi gave her immense pleasure.

After cordial greetings, Oma wanted to know why Käthe had come home midweek.

Käthe tried to form words, but they kept getting choked in her throat. Within moments, she had burst into tears. This upset Heidi, who had never seen her mother as anything but a happy songbird. Oma shuttled Heidi into the living room and gave her a basket of thread spools as play toys. Heidi usually entertained herself contentedly, imagining the spools as people, but after Oma went back into the kitchen, she crept to the doorway. She was in the habit of observing the grownups, who were often surprised when she repeated their words.

Oma had long realized that this girl comprehended what was happening in the adult world much more than other children her age.

For this reason, Oma lowered her voice so Heidi could not hear, but Käthe was losing her composure and raising hers.

"How could he? That *schweinehund*!" Bastard.

"Mind your language."

"I will not. And Lucy! My sister! How could she?"

The word "*Lucy*" came out of her mother's mouth with so much venom that it made Heidi retreat behind the door. She had never heard such anger from her mother.

Lucy was the youngest of three sisters in her mother's family. First came her mother, Tante Hedel, and then Tante Lucy, with her dark eyes and black ringlets—spoiled as the family favorite. Lucy was followed by their little brother, Heidi's Onkel Edward. This uncle was ten years older than Heidi.

Heidi strained her ears, and Oma seemed to plead, "I cannot choose between my daughters."

"Can't or *won't*? You would protect your precious Lucy. She has always been your favorite."

"That's not true or fair."

"Your actions speak. If you allow Lucy to stay in this house, then Heidi can't be here. She would turn my child against me."

Oma shushed Käthe, and they again lowered their voices.

Not long after this, Käthe stomped into a bedroom alone. Heidi wanted to follow her, but Oma retrieved the girl. It was time to pick up the bread.

When they entered the bakery, Heidi's mouth watered at the smell of fresh bread. She stared with fascination as the baker opened the iron oven doors, then slid the large loaves out with a tool that looked like a long-handled spade.

It made her think of open sandwiches with homemade cottage cheese, salt, pepper, and onions. They enjoyed this together most mornings when Opa came home from the coal mine on his bicycle. He never spoke to Heidi directly and sat on the men's side in church, away from the women. Although distant by nature, his arrival each day was a happy time.

The coal mine gave Opa a steady cash income as he also farmed a modest plot outside the village. While he was gone, Oma managed a kitchen garden behind the house with a small flock of chickens and geese. Heidi loved everything about farm life, especially the animals—baby pigs, best of all.

When Oma and Heidi returned home with the bread, Oma cut off the top crust, which she always gave Heidi because it had the best flavor. Then she spread it with rendered goose fat and garlic, and Heidi bit chunks of the chewy treat. Heidi could feel Oma's gaze as she ate.

Heidi asked about her mother, but Oma hushed the child. "Your mother is sad today," she said, making a fist and placing it over her heart. "You will keep with me."

Heidi did not leave her grandmother's side for the rest of the day, and her mother did not join them for dinner.

Then it had been time for Heidi to accompany Oma through the forest with Oma's friends. After they finished working on the goose quills, Heidi held Oma's hand all the way home—the girl had no more scamper left.

The forest lay in darkness now, and Heidi asked, "Where is the moon?"

Oma answered, "It sunk below the trees. You can count on the moon again tomorrow."

When they reached the clearing at the village edge, Heidi spotted the moon not entirely out of view, still clinging to the horizon.

She pointed up, "My friend is going to sleep."

Oma laughed with delight at Heidi's words.

Inside, they tugged off Heidi's boots and coat. She crawled into bed and fell asleep at once.

When Heidi awoke the following day, she heard Oma hauling laundry to the basement wash kitchen. Their family shared a three-story brick building with two other families, and tenants shared the basement for laundry where water for boiling sheets was heated by the coal furnace.

Heidi put on her cozy knitted socks made by Oma and stiff leather house slippers made by Opa. Their house had unfinished wood floors, so the family always wore these slippers inside.

She checked her mother's room, but the bed was already made, so she padded downstairs and pulled up a stool. Why had her mother gone out so early?

Oma's washtub was a new contraption lined with washboards on the inside. First, clothing went into the tub, and then a second tub had washboards lining the bottom. This washboard-bottomed tub nested atop the clothes. Oma worked a wooden handle back and forth, which agitated the laundry against the washboards. Every time the handle hit one side or the other, it made a sound, so for the better part of the morning, Heidi listened to the rhythm of click-click, click-click.

Oma wiped her brow, then rubbed a bar of lye soap on the fabric. When she finished each tub, she wrung the clothes and then hauled them up to the attic for stringing on lines spanning the rafters.

Heidi's mother appeared at breakfast with red eyes that gave away a night of crying. Then, she told Heidi to mind Oma and left the house in a coat and walking boots. "I have business to attend to."

A look of alarm crossed Oma's face, but she held her tongue in front of Heidi. Perhaps if Oma acted as if nothing had happened the day before, then the storm in their family would blow over.

After Käthe left, Oma was quiet for a long time but sought to reassure the girl. "My happy child. Anyone who brings such joy will receive it in return."

Later that afternoon, Heidi trailed Oma as they removed clothes from the lines, still slightly damp, and hauled a large basket down the street. Their destination was a shop where she would pay for use of the mangle to iron their clothes and linens.[4] Heidi loved how a wave of warm, laundry-scented humidity washed over them at the door.

Oma paid for the use of the large rollers that spanned whole walls. Heidi was amazed by the skill of Oma's hands as she fed each shirt or pillowcase into the roller, quickly

---

4   Heidi remembers it being pronounced "mungle," which seems to be a variation of the word "mangle," a piece of industrial ironing equipment such as Heidi described from memory.

pulling back her fingers before they could get caught in with the fabric. Then she tugged each piece out as it rolled from the top, steaming fresh. There was a certain soothing rhythm in the work for Oma—in any kind of work.

Before Oma could finish, Heidi looked up at the sound of the shop door opening hard. Her mother stood there out of breath. In a flash, Käthe had scooped Heidi up saying, "We must go."

Oma hastened to gather her half-pressed laundry, but Käthe was already out the door holding Heidi and walking fast. Heidi saw tears on her mother's cheeks.

Back inside the house, Käthe retrieved a small suitcase she had already packed, and the two were leaving as Oma got back. Oma begged her daughter, "Please don't do this. There is another way."

Käthe shook her head. "Everyone makes choices, and choices have consequences. I didn't choose this, but Heidi and I will make our own way now."

Käthe and Oma were both crying, which made Heidi do the same. Heidi took her mother's hand, and she looked back at Oma standing in the door. Oma's hands were clasped over her mouth.

Mother and daughter walked on snow-packed roads in the opposite direction from the town center. They made their way past the village shops and into the countryside. Käthe forced herself to be cheery, pointing out birds and animal tracks. This was the longest walk Heidi had ever known, and it felt like hours. Her mother sang songs to keep the girl entertained.

After a while, her mother told Heidi of a beautiful villa where other children would play with her. They stopped to rest on some rocks and ate bread and cottage cheese as a pallid winter sun drooped in the sky.

Soon after, they spotted a storybook villa with warm lights radiating from inside. It looked inviting, and when they came into view of the door, some smiling women dressed in religious habits hurried out to greet them. "Are you cold? Come in for coffee."

But Käthe declined the refreshment.

On the threshold, Heidi's mother knelt and hugged her. Then, she said, "Can you be brave and good, my little myszka?"

Heidi nodded. *Yes, she would.* She wanted to do anything that her mother asked.

Then her mother said, "I need you to stay here for a while. You will make me proud. Now I must go and make a life for us. I will come for you as soon as I can."

Then she stood, turned away, and walked toward the gates.

Heidi did not understand.

A sister crouched down to face the girl at eye level. She said in German, "You will stay with us at The Mother Eva House.[5] It will be good for you here."

Heidi's mother briskly walked away from the door, not looking back. She couldn't bear it.

"*Mútti!*" Mama! Heidi called out.

Once out of sight, Käthe slumped onto a tree and cried, hitting a gloved fist against the bark. She was growling as though to her husband.

---

5   The Mother Eva House was named for Eva von Tiele-Winckler. Mother Eva had been born into the wealthiest family of the region not far from Oma's village. She grew up, became a deaconess in a Protestant order, and subsequently founded more than forty "children's homes." The sisters' mission was to help shape the image of God in the child through educational activities and caring. They had a commitment to children with "sore little souls." They were known for working energetically and happily to form loving relationships with those in their care. Their wards included orphans and children whose families paid for boarding.

"Why? How could you do this to your daughter? You didn't have to see her face. No. You left that to me, you schweinehund. Are you still punishing me because our son got sick? Couldn't you see my grief? Selfish! Selfish! Selfish! I will never forgive you for this day."

Back at the villa, the sisters scooted Heidi indoors and tried to comfort the bewildered child. Heidi did not understand what was happening. Why was her mother leaving? Were they not going away together?

Heidi was used to her mother going to Berlin, but now tears streamed down her cheeks, and she shrieked.

"Why can't I go with Mútti? I want my mútti! I want Oma!"

One of the women took the girl's suitcase and helped tug off her boots.

"You will be cared for here as you were at home."

The woman then nudged Heidi up a flight of grand stairs, still crying but not fighting. A group of children sat in a large room, working on chalkboards. They turned to stare at the scene.

Heidi and one of the sisters entered a large room lined with beds along the walls. The sister sat Heidi down on a bed—her new bed. It had already fallen dark. They led Heidi to the toilet, a marvel since Heidi had never experienced indoor plumbing.

Then, the sister slipped off Heidi's stockings and dress. She pulled nightclothes over Heidi's head, and another woman entered the room. She knelt to offer Heidi a cup of warm milk, placing the girl's hands around it.

"Drink, child. Tomorrow will be a new day."

Other children filed in to get dressed for bed, said their nightly prayers, and the woman tucked Heidi into bed, staying until Heidi cried herself to sleep.

Heidi slept fitfully and awoke in the night to unfamiliar sounds of the big house creaking and children moving noisily in their sleep. When the sun rose, her eyes opened at the rustle of children getting out of their beds. She ached for home.

Heidi watched them go through their long-practiced routine. First, the children dressed and combed their hair, then returned items to little bags that hung at the foot of the beds. Soon, a sister came to help her out of bed, pulling clothes from her little case.

Heidi said, "Thank you, nun."

The woman smiled. "You may call me Sister. We are not Catholic nuns but belong to a Protestant order."

Heidi asked about her mother, but the sister gently shushed her and only said, "She went back to Berlin. You will be happy here."

Heidi followed the other children to a dining hall where they ate at long tables on benches. Then they broke into smaller groups with older children doing kindergarten activities and the children Heidi's age gathering for a story.

After lunch, they put on boots and walked the grounds for fresh air and exercise.

There were wooden toys, and tin wind-up toys unlike any Heidi had ever seen. Children gathered in small groups of similar ages to play games.

Heidi watched what the others did and copied. Then, a sister helped Heidi undress at bedtime and told her the steps the children would follow each night.

Heidi asked, "When is my mother coming?"

The sister answered with vague kindness, "She will come when she comes. You have accomplished your first day. Tomorrow will be easier, and the day after that better still."

The next day, the sisters assigned an older girl to help Heidi with the routine. Heidi soon learned to do the steps herself by following the other children. She dressed, walked in line to meals, and brushed her teeth.

She hoped for her mother, but the sisters tried to assuage the child. "Settle in, little one. She is not coming yet."

Many of the children were orphans—their parents would never be coming for them—but Heidi did not doubt that her mother would be back.

When children were disobedient, they had to kneel as a sister hit the backs of their feet with a brush. Heidi never wanted to receive that punishment, so she did not get in trouble.

The house kept strict discipline, but the sisters were also kind. Heidi learned to enjoy the busy activities they did together.

On March 12, 1939, the sisters told Heidi it was a happy day. Her stomach fluttered, thinking that she must be going home. "It is your third birthday." They baked a cake, and her Oma and Tante Hedel came to visit. They all had a little party and made Heidi feel special.

Tante Hedel and Oma brought a red velvet dress with rabbit-fur trim on the skirt. A matching hat framed Heidi's round face with fur, and her blonde bangs were combed in a straight line. They also gave Heidi the most beautiful doll she had ever seen, nearly half her size, wearing a white dress and matching bonnet. But Heidi did not really care for dolls. Instead, she longed for kittens and animals from the farm. Heidi was hoping to leave with the women and to be back with all that she loved.

They had photographs taken together to send to her mother, and then the two women had to go. Heidi was stricken with grief again, and her lip quivered, trying bravely not to cry. But she lost the battle.

■ ■ ■

Time passed, and Heidi was soon distracted by spring festivities, the first of which was Easter on April 9. For this holiday, the children and sisters celebrated by decorating eggs. These, they were taught, represented Jesus rising from the tomb.

Ten days later, the household began preparing for another holiday.[6] On the evening of April 19, they gathered around the radio to hear a speech from Joseph Goebbels. He was congratulating Adolf Hitler on his fiftieth birthday, to be celebrated by the entire nation the next day.

Goebbels said, "No German at home or anywhere else in the world can fail to take the deepest and heartiest pleasure in participation. It is a holiday of the nation, and we want to celebrate it as such."

The next day, the villa was draped in bunting, and the sisters raised a crisp red and white swastika flag. The children got special treats, and the household listened to a live radio broadcast of the pageantry in Berlin.

Announcers described the glittering scene: Spectators were seated in grandstands, and others lined the parade route dozens deep. Buildings throughout the city were bedecked in red swastika flags and golden eagles. Hitler Youth assembled in short trousers and neckerchiefs. Some 50,000 troops were to parade impressive new equipment

---

6   Hitler's fiftieth birthday party was declared a national holiday, and a military parade that lasted four hours served as a warning to other countries by flaunting Germany's military power. It was a lavish spectacle including some 50,000 troops along with tanks, planes, and groups of Hitler Youth. Several hundred thousand spectators attended, including 20,000 official guests. We do not know if Heidi's mother attended, but she was in Berlin at the time and enamored of the city, so she may have been there regardless of her political leanings.

and dress uniforms. Through the radio, the crowd could be heard chanting, "*Sieg heil! Sieg heil! Sieg heil!*" Hail victory!

The official motorcade approached the Brandenburg Gate, and when Hitler first emerged from his Mercedes tourer, onlookers hushed as he marched to the reviewing stand. Then, the children heard masses of people in Berlin erupt into cheers.

The country had not witnessed such a spectacle since the 1936 Berlin Olympic Games. The Olympics had occurred just months after Heidi was born when Käthe was twenty-two. She had listened to the radio with Heidi at her breast. After hearing all the glory from afar, Käthe made up her mind: She would find some way to get to Berlin.

Shortly after that, when Heidi was still a baby, Käthe auditioned for and received a scholarship at the State Opera (called the Staatsoper). This represented the opportunity of a lifetime. She would leave the muddy village and make her musical family proud.[7] Käthe could not anticipate then the jealousies to follow when she got out. Her next-younger sister Hedel soon trailed Käthe to Berlin, leaving Lucy to pick up the slack at home. If Lucy truly had been the family favorite in earlier years, Heidi usurped that role as the apple of Oma's eye. Three years later, Heidi was no longer in the care of family—a chain reaction.

Now, in 1939, other cause-and-effect forces were at work, but on a much bigger scale. The Führer's birthday parade was meant to show the world that Germany had risen beyond the shame of Versailles. They would finally triumph after years of economic and political uncertainty and the hardship of depression. Now, Hitler was making good on his promise to show Germany's greatness.

---

7   Germany had programs to scout talent from the hinterlands in science, athletics, and the arts. Käthe was just what they were looking for: a tall blond with pale skin, blue eyes, and musical abilities.

One of the sisters turned to Heidi, "Half of Berlin is there, maybe even your mother. It must be so exciting."

The sisters hushed the children so they could hear the Führer's speech. Then, the broadcasters described a procession of hundreds of military flags representing all the regiments, infantry goose-stepping in immaculate precision, and elite paratroopers, followed by motorized units and new tanks. It soon became tedious for the children, and the elder Mother Superior had her fill too.

She stood and clicked off the radio. Under her breath, she muttered, "They who take the sword shall perish by the sword."

She had lived through the last war, and when a young sister looked puzzled, Mother Superior sighed. "This is a parade to the glory of war. The way of Christ is peace. Christ said, 'Suffer the children.' These children are our charge. But what is a child to a tank? I'll tell you. An obstacle and nothing more. How soon we forget."

The children were thus spared from sitting for a parade that would extend for hours.

On a rainy day not long after that, Heidi felt restless and wanted to look out the window. The bedroom had tall ceilings and large windows with wide sills, but children were forbidden from climbing up there; a child might break the glass, or worse, fall through.

But when the sisters and the other children left the room, Heidi lagged. When no one was looking, she pulled herself up. There, she perched with her knees pulled to her chest entranced by the falling rain. Soon, however, she was startled by a voice calling, "Heidi?"

She would be punished, so she jumped down quickly. But her dress caught on a sliver and threw her off balance. Instead of landing on her feet, she tripped and held her arm out to break the fall. She crumpled into a heap, shrieking in pain.

The sister rushed to Heidi, whose arm was bent at an unnatural angle. Broken.

They called in a doctor who wrapped it in plaster. Heidi did not get in trouble. Rather, the pain of a broken arm, the maddening itch inside the cast, and having to sit out of activities was all the punishment she received.

A few days later, Heidi looked up to see her mother walking through the doorway. Heidi dropped her toy and ran to meet her with a rush of joy.

She was finally going home!

Heidi and Käthe enjoyed a picnic outside under blossoming fruit trees. When they went back inside, Heidi's voice was gleeful, "I will get my suitcase!"

But her mother shook her head. "Oh, no. Mała myszka, this was only a visit. I can't take you with me today."

Heidi did not understand at first. "I want to go with you."

Her mother again shook her head.

As Heidi grasped her mother's words, she flung her little body onto the ground and collapsed in tears and sobs. She flailed her cast, threatening to hit anyone who came close. Unlike the first time her mother left her there, now she knew what was happening. She had been bewildered then; now she was crushed.

That night she had a terrible dream. In it, her mother was dead, and Heidi felt abandoned and angry. All her family, the sisters, and others gathered around a large hole in the ground. Scary-looking men lowered a coffin containing her mother's dead body, and Heidi jumped into the hole with it, clinging to the wood, screaming and crying. They tried to pull the girl off, but nobody could pry her away. Dirt began to fall on her head just as she awoke.

Someone was shaking her because Heidi had been calling out into the room, "No! No! No!"

That was the first time she had this nightmare, but not the last—it would recur throughout her childhood.

After her mother's visit, she began wetting the bed, even though she had been potty trained for a long time.

Many months passed after that with no visits from her mother. Käthe had decided it was simply too hard on everyone for her to come. It only reopened the wound.

Heidi's homesickness subsided as she fell into the house's routine. She did like being there, and she was learning something new every day.

Heidi's favorite time of day was when they went for the afternoon walk. The sisters had large baby buggies that held four babies or toddlers at a time, and the older children trailed behind. The sprawling grounds had fountains and gardens, all enclosed by a stone wall. On pleasant days, they followed the path to an ancient oak with a swing hanging from it. In the shade, a curious old man with long white hair and a long white beard waited for them. He was missing a leg, and his eyes were watery, but they still twinkled. He told fairy tale stories to the children's rapt attention. He must have spent hours preparing his stories because he made little props—dolls and furniture—woven from long green stalks of rye. He used these to act out the scenes and afterward gave the toys to the children.

Then, on a hot August day, the sisters read Heidi a letter. Her mother was coming again! To Heidi's delight, the letter read, "I will be taking Heidi with me."

The sisters had received it earlier but held the letter until the day before her mother's arrival, knowing the impatience of a young child.

Her mútti was coming the next day!

The sisters coached Heidi to show all she had learned: to dress, brush her teeth, and mind her manners.

When Käthe arrived, the sisters gently motioned to Käthe to wait. When the girl bobbed a curtsey, Käthe gushed at her big girl and then the two became a tangle of kisses and nuzzles.

"Let's go to Berlin. It's time for us to be together now."

CHAPTER TWO

AUGUST TO SEPTEMBER 1, 1939:
BERLIN BEFORE THE START OF WAR

BEFORE SETTING OFF ON THEIR big adventure, Käthe paid the balance of what she owed the sisters for Heidi's care.

Then, the pair strode beyond the stone wall and into the countryside. Heidi had daydreamed of this day, and it had finally come. She was beaming. At first, Heidi wanted to hold her mother's hand but soon broke free, big girl that she was. She had grown so much in six months, speaking in complete sentences with clear diction.

Käthe marveled to watch her daughter and was happy to let her walk untethered as she balanced Heidi's little suitcase, a purse, and the doll.

"Come along; we mustn't miss the train."

Whereas their trip to The Mother Eva House had been on a snowy winter day, this time, they walked in the hot sun past farmers cutting rye. The men worked in groups with long-handled scythes while women paired up to thresh grain. Heidi especially liked the alternating rhythm of their flails and the satisfying jostle of grain that followed each hit: thwack-thwack, thwack-thwack.

Käthe pointed to large black birds gleaning grain behind the farmers. "Legends say a crow will protect your home from bad spirits."

At last, after many little stops to let Heidi rest, they reached the train platform. They had plenty of time before boarding. Once seated on the train, Heidi watched out the window with big black-cherry eyes.

"Tante Hedel can't wait to see you. She is waiting at our apartment."

"Tante Hedel?"

"I never had a chance to tell you. We're roommates now. She will help take care of you when I am at the opera."

When Hedel moved in with Käthe, it had solved one of two obstacles that had prevented Käthe from bringing Heidi to the city earlier. Namely, she needed help looking after Heidi while she was at work.

The other problem was money. Käthe had difficulty getting by on her own, but Alfred had just been conscripted into the German Army. Before this, collecting support from him had been problematic, but most of a soldier's pay was sent directly to the wife. This reliable income was enough to help them afford a two-bedroom apartment.

About two hours later, their train pulled into the capital. Nothing in Heidi's imagination could have prepared her for it. Heidi's world had been Oma's home and the forest, and The Mother Eva House.

To a three-year-old, every new experience is an unfolding mystery, but this train was bringing her into a new land that hardly seemed real.

Her mother brimmed with energy. "I can't wait to take you to the zoo. They have elephants, giraffes, and gorillas."

Heidi took in the large gray buildings, stately gardens, trolleys, statues, and people bustling about in fine clothes. There were soldiers everywhere with sharp-pressed uniforms and glittering buttons.

In the village, she had seen very few cars, but shiny vehicles filled these streets. Where were all the horses?

When the train approached Berlin's century-old station, the Anhalter Bahnhof, everything dazzled her, and Käthe read the wonder on Heidi's face.

"Just wait until I show you the opera house."

They disembarked, Käthe clutched the girl's hand, and they snaked through the well-dressed travelers. Everyone hurried to important places.

With the station's façade to their backs, they traversed the station to board the S-Bahn line. Through the S-Bahn window, Heidi marveled at double-decker buses and delivery trucks maneuvering through traffic. Vehicle exhaust burned in her nose, and she felt the rumbling sound change when they went over a trestle or bridge.

Within minutes, they had entered Alexanderplatz. This was the heart of the city, where everything was old and grand. Käthe jostled Heidi out the door, and a few steps later, they faced an impressive apartment building. Käthe announced, "Kaiser Strasse 17. This is home."[1]

Their building was made of gray stones and had four living floors, a basement, and a gabled attic. Above the front door was a balcony propped up by a statue of Atlas that seemingly held the building on his back. This once-posh apartment building boasted ornamental masonry and bay windows with stone ledges. The top floor had a balcony where someone's kitchen garden flourished with tomatoes, onions, and herbs.

Käthe hefted one of the carved double doors open, and the two climbed three flights of stairs. A cleaning lady and fellow residents kept the building spick and span, but a closer look revealed the trim and flooring to be shabbier than in the building's more fashionable days.

---

1   The whole area was demolished after the war, and the street no longer exists. However, WWII era maps of the city show the address and layout of the neighborhood to be just as Heidi remembers them.

Hedel was already waiting at the open door, and she heartily embraced her sister. The two were close, and Hedel hadn't liked being alone when Käthe was gone.

Hedel sized up the girl. "We need to get you fed."

The entire third floor had once belonged to one upper-class family, but it was now subdivided into two modest flats. Käthe led Heidi to the room the two would share. Hedel had her own bedroom, and they shared a small bathroom with a toilet and sink. The kitchen adjoined the living room and featured a *kachelofen*, a green-tiled wall oven fueled by hard coal. To Heidi, this apartment was impressive and modern.

She made a beeline to the living room's fancy bay window to take in the bustling street below. Instantly, Heidi had a new favorite place in the world. She would never know boredom while watching from up there. Heidi and her mother spent the evening in a shared sense of magic over the teeming city. They could finally make up for lost time.

The following day, Heidi went straight for the bay window to spy on the city below. Käthe only allowed Heidi to approach the bay window with supervision because it was unscreened, but every time her mother got busy, Heidi gravitated there.

The following afternoon, Käthe smoothed out her daughter's velvet-and-rabbit-fur dress, then heated a curling iron in the flame of their gas range. They were going to dine in a restaurant.

Heidi was fascinated by her mother getting ready. First, Käthe tested the curling iron on a piece of paper. When the paper scorched, she let it cool and then pressed in a new sheet. This time it turned golden brown, and Käthe did her own hair while the curling iron heated up again. Then she applied makeup.

While growing up in the countryside, Käthe had been made to feel like an ugly duckling—a pale-looking little thing. Whereas her youngest sister had attractive brown eyes and raven hair, Käthe was so blonde that her eyebrows were transparent, and she had snowflakes for lashes. But by the age of eighteen, she had grown a head taller than Oma, with a slender waist and shapely curves. She learned the art of eyebrow pencil and lipstick. Suddenly, she was a knockout.

Her height and stage training gave her a confident presence, at once feminine but self-assured, and she dressed well for her figure. When Käthe spoke, her voice had a velvet quality with flawless enunciation. The opera training had taught her to sing and project herself like a star.

After Käthe was ready, she made Heidi sit still for her turn. As she worked on Heidi's hair, Käthe gave instructions. "Remember your manners. Curtsey. Say please and thank you. Do not open your mouth with food in it. Use your silverware."

When her mother finished this work, bouncy curls framed Heidi's face.

Out in the city, Heidi wanted to examine everything, but her mother kept a fast clip and eventually scooped up her child. Käthe was unaccustomed to the pace of a three-year-old.

They went down a few steps to enter the restaurant, which was a fancy place. It had a little stage and a grand piano. Some nights they would feature a string trio or a pianist, but tonight they had a singer—everyone knew Käthe, and the wait staff fussed over the child. More than one person remarked, "She looks just like Shirley Temple."

Heidi had not yet experienced going to the movies, but she would soon.

When someone asked Heidi how old she was, Käthe had coached her to say, "Three years old and still single."

This made everyone laugh; it was Heidi's first taste of the spotlight. She reveled in the attention.

After dinner, a live band took to the stage and beckoned Käthe. The waitress kept an eye on Heidi, and the owner introduced Käthe as a rising star at the Staatsoper.

Käthe performed a few popular numbers, then closed with the famous aria from *Madame Butterfly*, "One Fine Day."[2] Patrons clapped with hearty adoration, and Käthe returned to the table.

They did not have to pay for their meal because Käthe could sing for supper whenever she felt like going out. Indeed, while Heidi had been away, she had taken the opportunity to perform on any suitable stage.

What a break the scholarship had been. If Käthe was to make something of her voice, there was nowhere better to be than the Berlin Staatsoper. This city opened every opportunity to an attractive blond who could sing. In turn, Käthe returned her love. She was crazy about the city, one of the most cosmopolitan places in the world. As they walked home later that evening, Heidi saw that her friend, the moon, had made his appearance above the buildings. She felt warm knowing he was there in the city, even though she did not see him as much.

During the following weeks, they fell into a routine of going out to fetch the day's bread, taking different routes so Heidi could see more of the city.

It tickled Heidi one day when they walked just a few minutes from their apartment to see the new Bärenzwinger, or bear pit. It was a concrete structure that had just opened with several bears in it. When people threw food to them, Heidi clapped, and Käthe explained, "Bears are the animal of Berlin."

The two made a habit of dining in restaurants. It gave Käthe stage practice, and they loved going out. When she

---

2   Although Käthe had a broad repertoire, this is the song Heidi most associates with the memory of her mother.

saved money on food, Käthe could afford extra things they needed.

Another day, Heidi and Käthe caught a tram from the Alexanderplatz commons. While there, Käthe turned her back to Heidi to read an announcement on an advertising column. When she swiveled around, her daughter was not there. She called out frantically until Heidi came running from among a group of children chasing each other around a statue.

If there is a loop, children will run it; if they are running, others will join. It was too much of a draw for Heidi.

Heidi was scolded for not staying with her mother, but her face had now turned upward at the statue. She hardly saw it earlier for all the running, but now Heidi gazed at the colossal statue towering above her, with one arm outstretched and crowned by a fortress on her head.

"Who is she?"

"Her name is Berolina, and she watches over the city. I like to think of her as my personal good-luck guardian."

The two then caught a yellow S-Bahn train to the Staatsoper. As they neared their stop, Käthe oriented her daughter. "We are on Unter den Linden. This is the city's main boulevard. Down that way is the Brandenburg Gate. You can't see it through all these pretty Linden trees, but it's not far. I will take you there, but not today."

Käthe enjoyed explaining everything to Heidi, talking to her as if she were a much older child. They approached the opera house's main steps as though on hallowed ground; Käthe's voice took on a reverent quality.

"The Staatsoper is two hundred years old. It was once the largest opera in all the land."

It looked like a Greek temple, with Corinthian columns supporting a portico with an epic sculpture in relief. Around the façade stood statues, each one sheltered by its own niche.

Käthe took Heidi through a door reserved for performers and gave her a private tour. None of the fairy-tale palaces of Heidi's imagination could have prepared her for the grandeur of all this gilded trim, the stage's velvet fire curtain, elaborately painted ceilings, and balconies stacked high, floor after floor.

Heidi's mouth gaped open, and Käthe whispered, "This is where I sing."

Käthe could see her daughter's face light up, grasping what this place meant. The moment was magical for them both.

Käthe's pride betrayed the truth that she wished to make her daughter proud.

Heidi was given some props to play with while her mother rehearsed. Eventually, she fell asleep under a rack of costumes with the garment hems brushing her little cheeks. The pair returned from their outing aglow. They were always in a jovial mood after going out, but especially this time.

■ ■ ■

A week later, on September 1, Käthe, Heidi, and Hedel ate their usual breakfast of hard rolls and cheese. On Saturdays, they also enjoyed a soft-boiled egg in a little cup. Käthe had perfect posture, like she had swallowed a ruler, and she gently cracked her egg. Hedel sipped hot coffee, as Käthe announced, "The zoo has half-price admission this weekend. Maybe this is our chance."

But this thought was interrupted by some commotion on the street below. Two old men talked loudly, and Käthe went to the open window. She heard one say, "Isn't one war enough for a lifetime?"

Käthe clicked on the radio, joining in the middle of an urgent-sounding state broadcast. It was punctuated with phrase like "German honor" and "force being met with force."

Hedel chewed the side of her fingernail, and Käthe stared numbly out the window.

When the news report finished, all color had drained from her mother's cheeks.

The women sat stunned and silent for some time. Heidi dared not break their attention.

Hedel whispered, "Mechtal is right on the border. *We are Polish.*"

Now Heidi must ask. "Mútti, what is it?"

Käthe remembered herself and stood. At once, her face brightened, and she projected confidence. "Oh, little mouse, there is no reason to worry. We are happy together, and that is all that matters."

But Käthe went to her purse, retrieved some money, and pressed it into Hedel's hands. "Go to the grocer and buy anything you can get—anything that will keep."

CHAPTER THREE

SEPTEMBER 1, 1939 TO DECEMBER, 1940:
THE FIRST INKLING OF WHAT WOULD COME

WHILE HEDEL WAS OUT, THE radio delivered instructions about blackout ordinances, effective immediately. Käthe rifled through supplies to comply with the requirements. One thing was clear. They would not be going to the zoo that weekend. It felt as though the sun had passed behind a cloud on a sunny day—a dampened mood had befallen the city.[1]

Käthe sensed how her child intently watched what she did throughout the day. Heidi often asked, "Mútti, what's that?" or, "What are you doing?" Heidi wanted to know everything and seemed to understand what was explained.

In response, Käthe developed a habit of narrating her actions for Heidi's benefit, which became an out-loud version of her inner thoughts.

At the bay window, Käthe took down the white curtains and said, "We have to take these down and hang ones that won't let light out."

She sucked in a deep breath through her teeth at the thought of blocking light, and placed her white linen cur-

---

1 Contemporaneous accounts described how residents of Berlin had a sickening sense of foreboding when they learned the news that day in 1939. Hitler had seemed sure that people would answer the rallying cry with vigor, but the horrors of the Great War were not so easily forgotten. Even many who supported the National Socialist Party were uneasy at the prospects of military conflict. For more on this, read Chapter 1 of Roger Moorhouse's *Berlin at War*.

tains into a basket with the rest of their soiled laundry. In the short time Heidi had been in Berlin, they had already fallen into routines that felt like forever to a young child. Each week, they carried it in a pillowcase to the Chinese laundry, which operated in a basement. Heidi always looked forward to the warmth and the smell of fresh laundry that hit her when they opened the door. It reminded her of going to the *mungel* with Oma.

Next, Käthe opened one of the matching suitcases she owned, which she used for storage when they were not traveling. She said with an exaggerated air of mystery, "Shall we see what's in this case?"

Hard-sided and with leather corners, Käthe had spotted the set in a secondhand shop. Like their apartment, the pieces were well-made and once belonged to upper-class people. To Käthe, they represented the allure of travel, and she wanted to own them. So, for the next few weeks after Käthe saw them, each time Käthe sang in a restaurant, she put a few pfennigs into a jar—the money she would have spent on the meal she received for singing. Soon, she purchased the set.

Käthe held up various items to show Heidi, "These are heavy stockings for winter. Oma knitted these mittens and scarf."

She placed a winter hat on her daughter's head. Heidi took in the smell of the Eau de Cologne her mother wore called "4711."

"I've never liked this scratchy blanket. It will do."

She held a wool blanket next to the bay window to measure whether it would cover the glass. It fit and was the right thickness to block light.

Then, she nimbly sewed a hem to hold the curtain rod and spread the blanket to give it a good brushing.

"This will keep moth eggs out."

As she worked, Heidi went to the radio and trailed her fingers across the wood case. This Blaupunkt tube radio had exquisite sound quality and was Käthe's most prized possession.

Usually, when news came on, Käthe switched to popular music sent from the BBC in London. Today, however, a commentator read a script of detailed instructions for achieving total blackout. It was something that any adults who survived the Great War would have been well-trained to do, but Käthe was only four when it ended, so she needed the information.

Heidi was bored and begged, "I want music, Mútti."

Käthe sighed in agreement. "I wish for that too, my little mouse. But no music plays today."

Heidi and her mother looked up when Hedel opened the door. "It's quiet on the street, but shops are busy. This is all I could get."

Hedel placed several sardine tins on the table and frowned.

The two sisters tuned in to a report of the German advance.

ON ALL FRONTS, THE EXPECTED SUCCESSES HAVE BEEN SCORED.

TROOPS ADVANCING FROM THE SOUTH, OVER THE MOUNTAINS.

SOUTH OF THE INDUSTRIAL DISTRICT, OUR TROOPS ARE ADVANCING RAPIDLY ON KATTOWITZ. THOSE FORCES ADVANCING FROM SILESIA ARE MOVING SWIFTLY NORTH-WARDS.[2]

The "industrial district" referred to the coal mines of their home region on the Polish border. When they heard

---

2   Roger Moorhouse, *Berlin at War* (New York: Basic Books, 2012), 207.

this news of troops marching, Hedel made the sign of the cross. "Mother Mary help us."

Käthe added, "Thank God Mechtal is on the German side."

Later that evening, another announcement sent a chill coursing down Käthe's spine. Listening to foreign radio would now be a crime punishable by imprisonment. She could go to jail for her BBC music habit. The announcer read the justification:

> IN MODERN WAR, THE ENEMY FIGHTS NOT ONLY WITH MILITARY WEAPONS BUT ALSO WITH METHODS INTENDED TO INFLUENCE AND UNDERMINE THE MORALE OF THE PEOPLE. ONE OF THESE METHODS IS THE RADIO. EVERY WORD THAT THE ENEMY SENDS OUR WAY IS OBVIOUSLY UNTRUE AND INTENDED TO CAUSE DAMAGE TO THE GERMAN PEOPLE. THE REICH GOVERNMENT KNOWS THAT THE GERMAN PEOPLE RECOGNIZE THIS DANGER AND EXPECTS THAT EVERY CONSCIENTIOUS AND DECENT CITIZEN WILL REFRAIN FROM LISTENING TO FOREIGN RADIO.[3]

Heidi was pulling on a nightgown as they heard a long howl sounding across the city, and Käthe went pale, "My God. That's an air raid siren."

Käthe wrapped her child in a blanket without changing, and they hurried out to the hallway stairs. Other residents were walking toward the basement. Enough people remembered bombardments from the Great War to know the routine, and they helped usher others underground. Remembering made them more uneasy about what the sirens meant, not less.

---

3   Michael P. Hensle, *Rundfunkverbrechen* (Berlin, 2003), 36–38.

Heidi looked up at her mother, and Käthe forced cheerfulness into her voice, "Let's go see what's in the basement!"

The procession was orderly—surely it was just a test of the system, right? In the makeshift basement shelter, people smiled, and some offered optimistic sentiments, but most were somber and uneasy. If news of war earlier in the day had not hit home, it was real now.

Within fifteen minutes, the all-clear siren sounded.

A man nudged his wife, "I told you it was just a drill."

The following day, Heidi saw a truck deposit sand in front of their building. Residents who had not known each other now gathered to fill hessian sacks with sand. Käthe and Hedel took their place sewing up the ends. Others worked to board up basement windows.

Soon, someone produced coffee, and another brought out a cake. The atmosphere was lifting considerably from the day before.

A neighbor who lived upstairs had two young children trailing her, a daughter a little younger than Heidi and a drooling toddler son who had a big smile but seemed slow.

She introduced herself as Frau Pohl and said, "Times like these bring out the best or the worst in people. It's good to see everyone coming together."

Workers applied phosphorescent paint to curbing throughout the city, and vehicles covered their headlamps except for a single slit of light pointing downward. Even flashlight lenses were painted with a blue filter. It felt surreal that their city was preparing for war, even as their leaders downplayed the action in Poland.

Later that week, Käthe unwrapped the paper from their clean, folded laundry. She sighed longingly and placed her pretty curtain into the suitcase where the blanket had been, "I hope we can hang these soon."

People soon adapted to the changes and tried to forget what was happening on the Polish front. No more air raid sirens sounded for a long time. Still, England had declared war against Germany, and that conflict was ongoing even though Poland had fallen, meaning that a certain tension hung in the air.

By December, the two sisters felt tremendous relief—along with the rest of the city—that the fighting was nearing an end. Germany now occupied Poland. Advancing troops had plowed through the region around Oma and Opa's village without stopping, since their village lay on the German side. It had been spared any destruction.

The Christmas holidays were an antidote to people's worries, and Käthe built up the magic of St. Nicholas Day on December 6. On the eve of the holiday, Käthe helped Heidi polish her shoes and set them on the windowsill for St. Nicholas to find. The next morning, Heidi was delighted to find nuts and candy there, eagerly unwrapping a piece. They set aside a handful of nuts to enjoy later.

Later in the month, Käthe took Heidi to a Christmas market, and they purchased a Christmas tree. These were in ready supply despite rationing of other goods. On Christmas Eve, Käthe, Hedel, and Heidi celebrated by hanging candles and fine strands of tinsel on the tree. Heidi's face lit up with wonder. She received a *Max and Moritz* book and another about Der Struwwelpeter. It was about an unkempt boy named Peter who never clipped his fingernails or cut his hair. She loved the colorful illustrations, and Käthe was like many other mothers who used it as an example of why a child must keep a neat appearance lest she be compared to Der Struwwelpeter. Because her mother often read it and then delivered a sermon about cleanliness, Heidi preferred it when Tante Hedel read to her. That is how reading the book became something enjoyable for aunt and niece to do together.

■ ■ ■

Heidi was not quite old enough to start playschool in 1940, so Käthe brought home a cat to help entertain Heidi. They named him Ivan, and he loved watching the city from the bay window as much as Heidi did. Ivan was a clever animal who walked the ledges of their building from window to window. Since it was winter, people set milk bottles out to keep cold. Ivan learned what was inside, and it did not take him long to figure out that he could topple the bottles and then lap up the milk. The neighbors threatened Käthe that they'd have him done away with if he kept doing it, but nobody ever harmed him. Heidi was smitten with Ivan, the first pet who was hers.

Rationing meant that everyone needed to economize, and part of how Käthe saved was to have lunch at Aschinger, one of their favorite restaurants situated near the Berolina statue at Alexanderplatz. There, Käthe ordered a bowl of pea soup and could fill up on the free rye rolls that were brought with it. Sometimes she took Heidi along, and they always tried to sit next to the big windows. Although the restaurant was beautifully decorated with chandeliers and other trimmings, Heidi always looked at what was happening outside rather than in.

Heidi did not witness a city at war that year, but rather, people going about their business as usual. The government continually assured the people that their anti-aircraft measures would prevent enemy planes from reaching the city, and there were no more air raids until a drill in March.

Then, on May 10, 1940, Germany invaded France. After Poland had fallen so quickly, the general mood in Berlin had quieted. This, however, was unsettling news. Although France was an old enemy, the government had repeatedly assured everyone that Poland was their only aim. Now this.

Shortly after that, it was Denmark and Norway. While people in Berlin somewhat understood the old rivalries with Poland and France, it was a troubling development to attack neutral Scandinavian countries. Hitler answered the criticism by barking about how the action was necessary to secure the northern flank and ensure supply lines.

Heidi overheard her mother talking to Tante Hedel about where Alfred, her father, was serving. Heidi was accustomed to her mother explaining things to her, but she sensed that this topic was off-limits.

Tante Hedel asked, "Why don't you divorce him?"

"If I had any self-respect, I would. But if he gets killed, then a widow's pension would help with the responsibilities he abandoned."

Her father was a foreign idea to Heidi. *Who was he? Why had he abandoned her?*

If Heidi ever asked questions, her mother gave terse answers.

■ ■ ■

The military escalation began affecting everyone in practical ways. There was heavy societal pressure for anyone who could work to do so. With so many of the nation's men serving in the military, foreign workers were brought in, and all unmarried women were urged to get jobs.

Initially, Käthe had coaxed Hedel to move in with her to help care for Heidi. It was, in essence, a nanny position for Hedel, who got free rent. But Hedel was bored and wanted more pocket money of her own. And so, one evening, Hedel delivered the news that she had secured a job in the nearby munitions factory. It paid well and would get her out of the house. Moreover, she reassured Käthe that she could still tend Heidi while Käthe was at rehearsals.

And then, as might have been predicted, Hedel's new job called her in early. This left a gap when their shifts overlapped. Käthe agonized over finding a solution but ultimately had no choice but to leave Heidi in the living room with a snack on the table. She locked the windows and gave her daughter strict instructions to stay away from them. Tante Hedel would be home in a few minutes.

Heidi often entertained herself quietly when the adults were busy, and she was not afraid of being left. However, she did not like having her freedom limited. So, as soon as Käthe left, Heidi unlocked the bay window, clambered onto the sill, and perched her little feet on a lip of stonework below.

Passersby reacted with alarm to see such a little girl alone up there. Heidi smiled and waved, and invariably, people smiled and waved back. Heidi found great amusement with this game.

After a while, Heidi spotted Tante Hedel walking home toward the apartment, so Heidi smiled and waved. Hedel almost dropped her bags as she ran toward the building.

For punishment, Hedel made Heidi kneel on dried peas. Her knees were red and hurting by the time her mother came home.

The next time their shifts overlapped, Käthe locked the windows and secured them with twine. As soon as the door closed, Heidi went to work on it. Soon, she loosened the knot and was smiling and waving at people below.

This time when Heidi saw Tante Hedel coming, she scrambled down quickly, but Hedel had still seen her. Heidi received the same punishment. Heidi's knees were still sore from before, and this time when it was over, they were puffy too.

The next time, Hedel tied Heidi's leg to the leg of the sofa with a sash, but Heidi worked her way out of that too. The peas hurt worse each time. But the moment she was left alone, she liberated herself.

Käthe gave Heidi a spanking for disobeying Hedel while swearing in Polish, but she never stayed angry for long.

Afterward, Heidi heard her mother and Tante Hedel discussing their inability to keep Heidi inside when they left.

Hedel went to her room and retrieved a letter from Oma. "She is begging you to send Heidi back there. Why don't you?"

"If Heidi and Lucy lived in the same house, Lucy would take her hatred out on Heidi, and you know it."

Hedel did not argue the point, and Käthe rubbed her temples with a handkerchief scented with Eau de Cologne 4711.

By summertime, France capitulated, and the soldiers came home to a lively victory parade. People had been waiting for this moment so they could return to normal. They had waited anxiously for the boys to come home, so the city went wild celebrating.

French champagne, brought back by soldiers, was suddenly available everywhere, so Käthe and Hedel got a bottle and had an at-home party. The women were in a laughing mood, and Heidi wanted to be silly too, so she found a clean, knitted menstruation belt and came out wearing it on her head, not knowing what it was. The sisters giggled and removed it.

Käthe became talkative when she drank and confided to Hedel, "With the boys coming home, I suppose it's time for me to file for divorce."

Hedel asked, "I never understood why you married him."

Käthe sighed, "Mother never told me anything about life. I was so naïve that I thought I would get pregnant after a heavy kissing session. He wanted more, and I didn't even know *what* yet, so when he proposed, I married him. I was trusting and dumb."

Hedel snorted.

Käthe added, "I wish Mother had explained these things. When my period first started, I didn't know what was happening. Someone in school pointed and said, 'There's blood on your skirt.' I thought I was dying."

Hedel said, "I'm glad I had you to tell me what I was in for."

Käthe nodded. "I will be different with Heidi. I will better prepare her for the world."

Käthe's mood took a contemplative turn, and a tear escaped her eye.

"Alfred was fun at first, but he was always controlling. He did not even want me wearing a swimsuit when we went to the beach. We had no hope of recovering after we lost the baby. I thought the pain would go away after we had Heidi, but it still hurts. I think of his tiny hands and feet...."

She trailed off with tears now streaming down her cheeks and excused herself to the window.

It was the first time Heidi heard that she wasn't the only child born to her parents. She had a brother who died? She could feel her mother's sadness, and it made her sad too.

Käthe stumbled into bed and found Heidi pretending to sleep.

During the week of August 20, 1940, British planes, or Royal Air Force (RAF), found Berlin. Air raid sirens called everyone underground for a short while as the RAF dropped a few incendiaries on a wide area around Berlin—mainly in the suburbs. It only lit a garden shed on fire and didn't hurt anyone. The authorities laughed it off as a fluke that would not happen again.

But a few nights later, on August 28, Käthe and Heidi were jarred from slumber by the wail of sirens. They didn't bother going to an official shelter and just huddled in the basement for three long hours. Heidi dozed, but Käthe didn't get a wink of sleep from midnight until 4 a.m.

About 150 small incendiaries had fallen in the city's first heavy attack. Official reports were that the damage was minimal, but the blow to public morale was not. For one thing, it had cost everyone a night's sleep, which made Käthe—and everyone—feel short-tempered.

More than that, people were stunned. It meant that enemy planes had pierced the outer rings of the city's defenses. The government had assured everyone that Berlin was the most protected city in Europe and that bombs would not drop on the city.

Reichsmarschall Hermann Göring had personally assured the people, joking that if a single enemy bomber reached the capital, then his name was not Göring; it was Meyer, one of the most common working-class names in Germany.

This bombing was a life-shifting moment for Käthe. She was already jaded after the military invaded France, followed by the Scandinavian countries. Now she doubted everything.

It wasn't hard for Berliners like Käthe to fall into disillusionment, as they had never been as enthusiastic as the government wanted to believe. Official mood reports had already given the propaganda minister reason for concern. The next day, one didn't need a report to gauge morale. People's faces showed their shock when they saw how bombings had taken out Görlitzer Station, left four-foot craters in a main thoroughfare, twisted tram lines, and destroyed some large houses. About 900 people were left homeless that night, and twelve lost their lives.

Those were the first air raid deaths of the war. Before that night, the war had been in Poland and France—elsewhere. The press derided England as barbarians for bombing a residential district. Hitler was outraged, saying:

And should the Royal Air Force drop two thousand, or three thousand, or four thousand kilograms of bombs, then we will now drop 150,000, 180,000, 230,000; 300,000, 400,000; yes, one million kilograms in a single night. And should they declare they will greatly increase their attacks on our cities, then we will erase their cities! We will put these night-time pirates out of business, so help us God! The hour will come that one of us will break, and it will not be National Socialist Germany.[4]

It had been almost exactly a year since Germany went to war with Poland, and now, war had come to the fatherland.

After that, when the air raid sirens sounded in the night—always at night—people took the danger seriously. Käthe and Heidi got plenty of practice that September and October, with air raids occurring on average about every other night.

Käthe generally kept her cool when getting to a shelter, but one evening they went to a large new bunker that had been advertised as having state-of-the art safety and many creature comforts. Masses of people zigzagged through narrow hallways far under the earth, as more waited outside, pressing to get in. Humans mashed together, carried along by the force of momentum. There were rooms off to each side, and at the open doors, people spilled into the rooms like cresting waves. The first rooms filled, and then the next, so they descended lower and lower. Käthe heard a terrible muffled sound of someone who had fallen under the mass, gurgling and drowning. She held Heidi for dear life until they finally came to an open room.

Käthe stayed calm, and so Heidi took cues from her mother, but inside their room that night, the noises and dust frightened Heidi. It also stank of body odor, people passing gas, and soiled baby diapers.

The next time there was an air raid, Heidi and her mother went to the U-Bahn station at Alexanderplatz. These stations were safe underground, and it was easier to duck inside. They were also more fun, with plenty of room for Heidi to run around. They even had little kiosks where

---

4   Moorhouse, *Berlin at War*, 141 (see his footnote 23).

people could buy something to eat, beer, or a newspaper to read. After that, Heidi looked forward to the U-Bahn stations because it was a chance to play with other children.

Heidi and her mother continued going out to sing at least once a week. Then, one evening in October, they went to a fish restaurant at the S-Bahn Bahnhof. As they approached the station, they saw some families with children. The children had placards around their necks with their names and destinations.

Heidi asked, "Where are they going?"

Käthe said, "To the countryside."

"Why, Mútti?"

"For safety during the air raids."

Heidi's black cherry eyes opened wide, "Will I have to go back with Oma?" Heidi missed her Oma, but she most wanted to be there with her mother.

Käthe said, "No. We will stay together here."

At the restaurant, Heidi studied the waiters wearing white gloves and diners smartly dressed for travel.

Then, her mother took the stage with her accordion and sang "Lili Marlene" in the same key and style as Lale Andersen. This had become the most requested song in her repertoire even after Goebbels, the propaganda minister, banned it from the radio. Maybe especially then. She started doing her hair like Andersen when they went out too, and Heidi overhead someone ask, "Is that Lale Andersen?"[5]

She thought, "No, that's *my mother!*"

Fall turned into winter, and Käthe's divorce became final.

---

5   This iconic song was first performed by Lale Andersen in 1939 and became popular worldwide during the war. Later, the German-born singer and actress Marlene Dietrich became synonymous with that song. Käthe learned to sing it like her too. During those early years of the war, Dietrich was working in America and would rally the troops from that side, but her version became the theme song on the German Language station of the OSS (US Office of Strategic Services), which had a Morale Operations Branch. Dietrich worked for this branch of the military.

The air raids eased up in November and December, and for Christmas of 1940, Käthe was finally ready to go home for the holidays.

Oma smothered her granddaughter with hugs and kisses, and Heidi reveled in the softness of her body. Returning to the village brought her memories flooding back.

Heidi, now a big girl at four years old, was eager to help Oma with Christmas Eve dinner. Oma showed her the steps of making bread pudding while she caught up on the latest from Käthe and Hedel.

First, Oma unwrapped stale bread she'd been storing in linen and soaked it in a mixture of eggs, milk, sugar, ground poppy seed paste, raisins, and a dash of almond flavoring from a tiny glass bottle.

As the bread sopped up the liquid, Oma asked Käthe, "Do you hear from Alfred?"

Heidi looked up with intense curiosity at hearing her father's name, and Oma diverted her attention by handing her a wooden spoon. "Stir," she said.

Käthe then answered sharply, "Don't say his name. He is still in the Army, but we do not hear from him. Mother, I have been granted a divorce."

Oma changed the subject by opening a jar of pickled pumpkin chunks. She handed a square to Heidi, who held it between her finger and thumb and smelled the cloves. The sweet-and-sour flavors exploded onto her tongue, activating her saliva glands. She bit into the firm, meaty cube and savored it like candy. Then, her molars crushed a whole clove, and the spice stung her tongue. She smiled anyway.

It was late afternoon, and Oma had Heidi help her with a trip to the root cellar. Heidi loved being outside again with the chickens and geese.

Inside the cellar, Heidi grinned an expectant smile, and Oma scooped sauerkraut from the barrel, then mashed down the cabbage and ladled extra juice for Heidi. As Heidi slurped, Oma fished carrots from a crate of damp sand.

Back inside, smells washed over them: roasted goose stuffed with chestnuts, apples, prunes, and onions; goose-fat gravy; and baked pudding.

Opa trudged down from the attic bearing a box of tree trimmings. A Christmas feast had been possible because of his long nights in the coal mine, followed by tending the animals and farm by day. Oma's frugal economy ensured they always had necessities. Other regions were suffering mightily from shortages of everything,[6] but their area was critical for the war and an export economy made many necessities—and even some luxuries—easier to come by.

They gathered around the live tree and pinned it with aluminum candle holders that they called tree frogs. They sang along with Käthe's accompaniment on the accordion. Then, when the time came to light the sparkling candles, Käthe played "Silent Night" on her tabletop zither. It sounded like a heavenly harp, and the family sang along.

Heidi received gifts of knitted clothes and a toy horse. She curtsied after receiving each one. "*Danke schön*," she said.

As they enjoyed dessert, Oma told Heidi, "Don't eat too much. Poppy seeds make you dumb."

Then, Oma opened a Bleigießen kit, a box containing lead toy soldiers. Each person took turns taking a soldier. They put it onto a spoon with a wooden handle and held it over a candle flame. Heidi was mesmerized as her soldier liquified. They poured their melted metal into a bowl of iced water. After it hardened, they placed the lumpy form

---

[6] Throughout Germany, ration allotments were theoretical at best. If one were to evaluate the nutritional intake available to a family through ration coupons, it would seem that nobody was faring terribly. However, redeeming the full measure of those coupons was generally not possible. This is one reason those in the countryside did so much better; subsistence was available from nearby farms. Source: Moorhouse, *Berlin at War*.

on Oma's outstretched palm. She inspected it and read the shape to give a prediction for each person in the coming year.

When it was Heidi's turn, Oma said, "It is in the form of a child. You will make friends this year."

When she got to Käthe's lump, Oma saw a backpack and a heap of clothes. One drip solidified into a long piece that looked like a gun, and there was a separate half-bubble of lead in the water. This piece reminded Oma of a helmet, and she placed it atop the weapon.

She said, "It is a soldier's clothes, gun, and helmet." Then she predicted, "Something is going to happen to Heidi's father."

Käthe rolled her eyes at the mention of Heidi's father, but Heidi looked concerned. Käthe laughed and said, "It's just a game, my little mouse. Nobody believes in these superstitions."

But Oma was serious about it.

Heidi soon forgot about the fortunetelling and went to sleep happy. After she tucked into her former bed in the kitchen, the adults slipped out for midnight mass.

When the holiday ended, Oma once again begged Käthe to leave Heidi there. Everyone in the house seemed to agree with Oma, but Käthe wouldn't hear of it. Once she was set in a direction, Käthe could not easily be changed.

"The safest place for the two of us is together. Our life is in the city."

CHAPTER FOUR

JANUARY 1941 THROUGH MID-1941: AN EVENING WITH HITLER

ON JANUARY 1, 1941, KÄTHE called Heidi to the window to see the city blanketed with thick snow. Children frolicked and pulled toboggans through the streets. Käthe took Heidi to the Tiergarten and let her play with others who had come with sleds and skates.

However, the fun wore off in the coming weeks as temperatures plummeted and trains froze to the tracks. The opera was canceled due to weather, and getting food became an all-consuming endeavor because the stopped trains meant a coal, potato, and vegetable shortage.

Inside, they layered their clothes with winter coats, hats, and gloves. Hedel, Käthe, and Heidi moved their beds into the living room and pushed them together to conserve heat. Layered under all the blankets, they huddled together. Heidi brought Ivan the cat under the covers, and Käthe worried he might suffocate with so many blankets.

Heidi cooed, "You must be the warmest creature in this city."

When they awoke to air raid sirens, they exhaled frosty puffs of breath. Shivering, they put on their clothes and went into the basement. They couldn't brave the frigid temperatures to get to a bunker.

Europe was experiencing the harshest winter in a century.

As Käthe made the day's ersatz[1] coffee, she was bleary-eyed from being up half the night and yearned for the real thing. Bone tired and bone cold, she and Heidi huddled by the stove. Ivan stayed indoors, and Heidi held him to her like he was a fur muff, purring at her warmth.

So, for the rest of the day, they sipped hot water for warmth. It was strictly forbidden to heat apartments with cookstoves because some people were asphyxiated, but Käthe didn't have fuel to spare anyway.

Churches, schools, factories, and restaurants closed because they did not have coal. The bitter cold made that winter feel endless, and summer days seemed as unreal as a fairy tale. If summer were a fairy tale, they had entered the dark part of a story, as though a spell had plunged the land into eternal winter. Käthe's mood veered into the type of superstition that her mother might believe. Had the war itself brought this punishing winter? It wasn't unlike some story where an evil force had cast a spell of darkness that would not lift until the fighting ended. She shivered and willed herself back to the present.

Smiling at Heidi, she announced, "Today is bathhouse day!"

"Can we go now?"

"Our time isn't until 2 p.m."

Their twenty-minute appointment was the best part of the week because they'd get warm to the bones, if only for a few minutes.

When they went out, they read official notices posted throughout the city:

NOBODY SHALL HUNGER OR FREEZE

---

[1] Ersatz means "substitute," and there would be plenty of improvisation through the war. Coffee was made from chicory roots when that was available. When that ran short, they had roasted barley, soybeans, or other grains sometimes mixed with molasses. The German government had programs to come up with substitutes for just about everything including leather, gasoline, rubber, textiles, and food.

Heidi heard Käthe snort under her breath, "And the punishment for disobedience?"

Käthe stretched out other highlights of their routine so they had something to break the monotony of their days—dropping off and picking up clothes at the Chinese laundry, for example. While going out wasn't pleasant, stepping inside that warm establishment was a welcome reprieve.

The daily bakery run was a mix of pleasure and pain. The queue meant they had to stand outside most of the time, but they were rewarded when their turn came to step inside. The bakery smelled heavenly, and the ovens gave off heat. This baker's hard rolls always tasted good. They had heard of poor-quality bread with the texture of sawdust, but he must have had reliable sources for ingredients. Their neighborhood was known for being a place where one could get things.

By February, the trains thawed, and snow slid off the roofs in sheets. The city warmed up by Heidi's fifth birthday in March. This milestone meant she could start playschool (kindergarten), a great relief to Käthe to now have a safe place for Heidi to be during the day. Money from Alfred's paychecks covered the tuition.

After being cooped up that winter, starting kindergarten was especially thrilling to Heidi. There was plenty of unstructured time to explore the yard or draw with colored pencils.

It was also the first time since being in The Mother Eva House that Heidi could enjoy extended playtime with other children and the same ones each day.

Shortly after starting playschool, Heidi had a creative idea. She organized a group of children into a line and gave each of them a haircut. When a teacher saw this, she intercepted their fun and gave Heidi a spanking. When Käthe picked Heidi up that afternoon, Käthe received a stern lecture from the teachers about teaching Heidi to obey the rules. Käthe frowned at her daughter and made her apologize.

Heidi wondered why she always did the wrong things. Getting in trouble like this brought back the time at Oma's house when she had another creative idea. She painted Tante Hedel's white walls with mud, and Hedel punished her by making her pick stinging nettle for their dinner—with her bare hands. It left red welts. Nettles were part of their diet, thrown into a pot like spinach, and cooked to neutralize the tiny plant hairs that sting. Heidi hadn't cared to eat any that day.

Käthe had a brisk walk when she needed to work out frustrations, and Heidi had to run to keep up. But it was hard for Käthe to stay mad at her little girl on such a beautiful day. Although many of the city's flowering trees had been cut down that winter for fuel, the remaining ones were now in bloom. Käthe felt more alive than she had in years. The world had thawed around the same time that the bombardments eased. The past few nights, they basked in glorious sleep. She was back to work and had a new date for that weekend. She exuded energy and decided to meander through the city to see what had changed since their last outing.

They boarded a tram, and once seated, Käthe asked Heidi, "Why did you cut those children's hair?"

Heidi shrugged defensively. "I don't know, Mútti." It was an honest answer—she didn't have words to explain why it had seemed like a fun game at the time.

"You must ask permission before doing things like that. There are rules and consequences."

But now Käthe's voice had the sound of playful imagination as she said, "Maybe you were practicing to be a grownup. I think that is what kindergarten is for, to play-act who you will become. Would you like to cut people's hair one day?"

Heidi marveled at her mother for understanding. Heidi knew she would not be punished further for the incident.

The two of them gaped out the window at the damage along Unter den Linden, and they got out to see the latest at the Brandenburg Gate. The entire structure had been draped in camouflage and foliage to disguise it from the air.

They made their way home, stopping to walk through the zoo park. Now that it was spring, a new construction site dominated the park. A staggering number of foreign laborers scrambled about, taking shrill orders from superintendents who oversaw the work with an air of military authority. These workers had been brought in from other countries to make up for the absence of men away fighting. They filled the large factories, and some of the more favored Czechs, Danes, and French workers were chosen by shopkeepers. Those were the lucky ones.

The unfortunate souls here were probably from Russia and Poland, or they may have been Jews. They stooped with the burden of labor, caked with dust. They never looked up, like doing so might invite a whip. Käthe didn't see a whip, but guards were positioned at intervals. They seemed to be prisoners of war and not volunteers.

What were they building? It seemed like a concrete monstrosity. Käthe had read in the paper that the structure would have a sophisticated anti-aircraft flak tower on top and bomb shelters within its depths.[2] She wanted to feel comforted by these protective measures but couldn't shake a foreboding feeling. She, like everyone, hoped that the worst

---

[2] Berlin's extensive bunker system and sophisticated anti-aircraft weaponry saved countless lives during the war. A total of eight flak towers were built in the city. These were large, concrete towers for defense against air raids, virtually impenetrable and containing radar, gunners, and shelters underneath. The zoo flak tower also became the repository for artifacts from the Berlin Museum. While many Berliners went into their basement cellars, the purpose-built bunkers were the safest. U-Bahn stations offered a more pleasant alternative.

was behind them. Paris had fallen, and they were breathing again now that the bombardment had subsided.

If war was behind them, why was this structure needed? Propaganda reports assured the people that these were only being built from an abundance of caution, yet construction of the city's defense was happening before her eyes. This defense appeared massive in scale. They had been told enemy planes would never reach the capital city, and yet, the latest bombardments had been terrible. If they ever needed this structure, they were in real trouble.

Käthe had heard of plans to make Berlin into a model city called Germania, something of a new Rome. So, was this it? Was this ugly building the vision that Hitler and his favored architect, Albert Speer, had in mind? If Käthe were to imagine her ideal city, this certainly wouldn't be it. This structure was ugly in every sense, the way it looked, the way it was being built, and what it meant—their city was carving out a portion of their beloved zoo to make a fortress. They were trading a park for defense that was only needed because of war.

Other passersby were basking in the glorious day. If they paused to watch the construction, they seemed approving. But that's what people must do—one did not attract attention. One did not criticize in public. *Sieg Heil.*

The construction work was fascinating to Heidi who wanted to keep looking, but Käthe couldn't stand any more of it. "Let's go," she told Heidi.

By the time they got home, Käthe had mostly shaken a feeling that she was covered in dust from the construction, that she had gotten dirty by watching. She brought herself back to the present.

She opened the mailbox on their way into the building and found an official notice and an accompanying red card.

It read that all radios, old and new, were to have the card attached. The card read:[3]

> REMEMBER. LISTENING TO FOREIGN BROADCASTS IS AN OFFENSE AGAINST THE NATIONAL SECURITY OF OUR PEOPLE. BY ORDER OF THE FÜHRER, IT WILL BE PUNISHED WITH SEVERE CUSTODIAL SENTENCES.

Käthe snorted, but the decree also chilled her.

"What is it, Mútti?"

"*Der mist.*" Dung pile. "Just something for the rubbish bin."

Käthe thought better of tossing it, however. It was an order, and she mulled over what to do with it. And so, instead of throwing the red card away or affixing it to her radio, she simply slid it underneath.

Hedel had been getting ready for work, and she now approached her sister.

"Can we have a word?"

Käthe's heart skipped a beat—it sounded serious, and Hedel's cheeks were blotchy like she was nervous. It seemed like Hedel had been waiting for them to come home.

Hedel began, "You know I've been seeing Franz."

"Yes. I am happy for you."

Hedel had been dating a Czech named Franz Franke who had grown up in a small town called Jägerndorf in the Czech countryside of Sudetenland. It was only about an hour from their village, and the pair of sweethearts had much in common.

Hedel's aquamarine eyes were the same color as Käthe's, and they sparkled against the contrast of her black hair. "He asked how I would feel about living in the countryside."

---

3   Moorhouse, *Berlin at War*, 213.

"Did he ask you to marry him?"

"Not yet, but I feel he will."

Hedel explained that he worked for the railroad and was seeking reassignment back in his hometown.

Käthe joked with her sister. "You'd leave all this luxury?"

Hedel laughed.

"I see it in your eyes. You have missed the countryside. And love is love."

Hedel nodded in gratitude, accepting it as her sister's blessing.

Käthe and Hedel would always be close, but the two were of a different stamp, and Hedel was more at home in a village than the city.

With Heidi in playschool now, her help was no longer imperative. Käthe would make do, grateful for her sister when she had been needed most.

Ever since Hedel had been working and spending time with Franz, they were not spending as much time together anyway. Käthe had broadened her circle of artist and singer friends, including a woman named Lizzie Lupinski from Poland. However, these were not Hedel's people.

As Hedel grabbed her things and headed out, a knock came at the door.

"That will be Lizzie."

Hedel rolled her eyes. "That girl is *trouble*."

Käthe joked as she opened the door. "You mean free-spirited?"

Lizzie stepped inside with a baby on one hip while her other arm did an over-exaggerated "Heil Hitler!" Käthe pulled her inside. "Shhhh!"

Lizzie rolled her eyes. "What? It's the national greeting."

Hedel shuffled past Lizzie with a polite nod but shot back at her sister. "My point exactly. *Trouble!*"

Once the door closed, Käthe giggled, and Lizzie pulled out a small blanket and toy and set them on the floor.

Käthe called to Heidi, "Come and play with Wolfgang."

Heidi complied, trying to get him to giggle or say words while she watched her mother and Lizzie make fun of the Führer. She snickered when they slipped into Polish swear words.

Lizzie had descended from Polish aristocracy, and the two become fast friends after meeting among a network of artists and stage performers. Lizzie's primary occupation seemed to be finding men of status to date so she could marry well. This is what she had been reared for in life. Her parents had been increasing the pressure to find a husband, threatening to cut off her lifestyle.

Both women were twenty-seven and they still attracted plenty of attention—and both enjoyed it. Whereas Käthe turned heads with her statuesque presence, Lizzie was a petite brunette with a spunky personality. Käthe had a quick wit and cutting sense of humor, to which Lizzie responded with an effervescent giggle. Naturally, others wanted to join in if the two were involved in anything.

When they went out together, they often received interest from men. They understood each other as they were both single mothers of Polish background. Still, Lizzie faced more outward judgment from people in Berlin than Käthe, who seemed German in every way. Lizzie carried several stigmas as an unwed mother with a Polish last name and her son Wolfgang who had skin the color of coffee and milk. His father had been a traveling performer, but Lizzie didn't talk about him. He had long since exited the scene, perhaps not even knowing he had a son. He would never re-enter the picture. This situation had scandalized and frustrated her parents.

Käthe would often date a man once or twice, but she had been so hurt by Alfred that if a man got too serious about her, she'd tell them she had a child. This usually scared them away because most men she met wanted to date a beautiful and fun woman, but they'd exit if there was any "baggage."

Beneath the laughter, however, Lizzie was seething about the state of the world. Her mother and extended family suffered under German occupation that extracted their resources and aimed to push them into a lowly status. There was a pecking order, and Poles were only a step above Russians, with Jews, Romanis, and homosexuals beneath them all.

Käthe and Lizzie did not find it hard to make friends with people who shared their views privately. Hitler had never won more than 30 percent of the popular vote in Berlin. His Capital City was the least Nazified of any part of the country, not a stronghold of the National Socialist Party.[4]

Käthe had news for Lizzie, but she hesitated to share. However, she knew that Lizzie would learn about it eventually, so she might as well hear it straight. "I had lunch with someone new this week."

Lizzie wanted details, and Käthe obliged her curiosity.

She had caught the attention of a Wehrmacht officer named Werner,[5] after an opera performance and rebuffed him at first. It was common for soldiers to flirt with her because the Staatsoper was near the Reich Chancellery and was a particular favorite of Nazi functionaries and military officers. For a long time, she had been able to avoid involvement with these men by stating that she was married.

Word got out that she was divorced now, however, and she could no longer use her marriage as an excuse.

---

4   Moorhouse, *Berlin at War*, 271.
5   Werner is his real first name, but Heidi does not know his surname.

When this good-looking officer asked her to lunch, she said, "I'm a singer and have no interest in politics."

He replied, "I am a soldier with no interest in politics. Have a meal with me, and we'll only talk about music."

She understood that there was a difference between Wehrmacht military men and the dogmatic SS.[6]

She agreed, and at lunch, she learned that Werner was a career Army officer assigned to work on the personal staff of Magda Goebbels, the propaganda minister's wife. Käthe was naturally curious about Mrs. Goebbels but refrained from asking on that first date.

In studying him across the table, she surmised that Werner's assignment to the staff of Mrs. Goebbels had been because of his capabilities. He had the manners, personality, and intellect to be a pleasant and competent addition to her household. Moreover, Werner was a tanned and fit specimen of a man. He had been well-educated, too.

Although his position made him appear like an insider, he regarded the Army as a career, not an ideological mission. He had come from a military family with a strong tradition of career service, and his sworn duty was to his country. He had a job to do. However, Werner's real passion was music, and his attraction to Käthe began with this.

Käthe confided in Lizzie, "I like him."

Lizzie was skeptical. "Be careful. They're all pigs."

Werner asked Käthe to go out again, and they began attending performances together, went to art galleries, and

---

[6] Although Werner was an officer by the choice of his career, it was not uncommon for members of the Wehrmacht to be politically neutral or to differ in their views from the Nazi party. Werner had likely been on this path long before the current regime. It is noteworthy that it was high-ranking members of the Wehrmacht who would attempt Operation Valkyrie, an assassination plot on Hitler's life in March of 1943, calling the concentration camps a disgrace on Germany. In contrast, the Schutzstaffel or SS operated directly under Hitler and was responsible for enforcement and genocide. They were regarded as the Nazi party's elite unit. They would be feared and known as brutes throughout Europe.

sampled the many cultural opportunities available in Berlin. He was polite to Heidi and his salary could afford whatever they wanted to do, and a babysitter, too.

One day he came to the apartment with a bag slung over his shoulder.

When he entered, he closed the door quickly, and she inquired playfully, "Did you bring me some potatoes?"

He responded playfully. "Something better."

"Wine."

"Not today. What I have is better than that."

"No such thing."

"Just wait."

When she was seated, he fished out a box wrapped in newsprint. She examined it slowly to prolong the suspense and felt that it had some heft. When she removed the paper, she saw a Wehrmacht-issue radio.

"Don't you like the sound of mine?"

"Keep yours for music and propaganda. This is shortwave. With this, you can hear the country's secrets. It might save your life one day. It will tell you if bombings are coming, and from where."

She was stunned. "Where did you get this?"

"Work. Mrs. Goebbels has stockpiles of anything you could want. It will never be missed."

"But if it is discovered missing? This could cost you your job."

He grinned, "Or my head."

She shuddered. And was genuinely touched. "You did this for me? How can I ever repay you?"

"I have a few ideas. But before anything else, I have a request. I need you to come to dinner with me. It's a formal affair at the Reich Chancellery. There will be delicious food, and you'll get your wine."

Käthe flushed. It sounded delightful to dress up and go out.

"What's the catch?"

"The host. You're not a fan. The Führer himself will be at the head of the table."

"Oh, my."

"Come with me. I can't refuse. And it will be good for us to be seen there together."

Käthe accepted. It might be good for her career, and how could she pass up the chance to see inside the Chancellery and meet their country's leaders in person? She wouldn't mention it to Lizzie until later.

She did some window shopping for fashion inspiration. Even if she had extra money and ration coupons, the dresses in windows were only for show. If one inquired inside to purchase it, a shopkeeper would say that the outfit would only come available for sale once they changed it out. But the displays never changed. While she was out, she brought her silk stockings to a woman who mended a tiny run for a few pfennigs.

Käthe decided she would modify a black crepe dress she already owned. She removed the sleeves and replaced them with straps. Around her shoulders, she draped a fox stole that clasped at the mouth.

She grasped the nuances of the occasion, having observed party officials and military men at the opera with their wives. Wives of party men would be well-dressed and perfectly coiffed. As someone from the opera, Käthe could bare her shoulders, but good taste during a war meant not veering into the ostentatious. While Mrs. Goebbels had high-fashion sensibilities, junior-ranking military personnel took their cues from Hitler, who was known for having spartan tastes. Thus, Käthe sought to strike an appropriate balance for the evening—femininity and allure, with a mindfulness of the times.

Werner and Käthe took the tram, and she filled her lungs with the scent of tree blossoms. Even with city noises, she heard what must have been millions of honeybees having a party in the branches.

Inside the Chancellery, Käthe and Werner were escorted into an elegantly appointed room with high ceilings, an enormous crystal chandelier, and marble Corinthian columns. The evening began with a reception for mingling, and the long table was already set with elegant dishes and white linen for fifteen couples.

At 8 p.m., the guests were invited to their seats. The men helped women with their chairs, and when Hitler entered the room, guests stood until he took his place at the head of the table. He was accompanied by Mrs. Goebbels, whose husband would not join them that evening.

The propaganda minister, Joseph Goebbels, was Hitler's political right-hand. He personally wrote many of the speeches and managed the elaborate events held by the National Socialist Party. He and his wife, Magda, were regularly photographed with their six children, and Magda's eldest son from a prior marriage. She was the model German mother, devoted to her family and to the cause. She often stood beside the Führer at state functions since he was unmarried.

Despite public appearances, Käthe heard rumors of the many affairs Joseph Goebbels had, and the jokes that made the rounds about his appetites. She couldn't help but wonder about the private thoughts of this elegant woman at the head of the table. For the evening, Mrs. Goebbels had assumed the title she was regularly given as "First Lady of the Reich." What does any first lady think in private? What must any woman do to keep appearances? How often did

Mrs. Goebbels dine like this? Was it always a treat, or did it become wearisome?

Mrs. Goebbels smiled, laughed, and talked, but she looked tired.

They were served courses of a sumptuous vegetarian meal with wine—apparently the whole affair was unrestricted by rationing. Hitler was avid about not eating meat, believing humanity's future depended on this diet.[7] Thus, the vegetable dishes were varied and delicious. While the others sipped on wine, the extent of Hitler's alcoholic consumption was a glass of his special low-alcohol beer. It was well-known that he abstained from drinking, smoking, and eating meat. It wasn't well-known, however, that he suffered from stomach distress, which affected what he could eat and drink.

Between courses, the companions were each introduced, and the Führer looked at Käthe, made eye contact, and nodded his head in seeming approval.

Lively conversations ensued around the table, and Hitler spoke little. Instead, he listened as though soothed by the cacophony as one might be soothed listening to waves crashing onshore. When Hitler did speak, his voice was calm and without the agitated overtones that punctuated his radio addresses. He ate more quickly and methodically than others at the table, as though performing an exercise routine. However, he did not rush the meal, which took about two hours.

Music played from a phonograph during dessert, with Hitler choosing the selections. He was an avid connoisseur of the opera, a favored profession in Reich circles.

---

7   "Adolf Hitler and Vegetarianism," Wikipedia, accessed August 17, 2024, https://en.wikipedia.org/wiki/Adolf_Hitler_and_vegetarianism.

Although Käthe had no interest in joining the National Socialist Party, she couldn't help but find the evening thrilling and would certainly never forget it.

A few days later, on the night of April 9, a big air raid hit. The spring had been mostly quiet, but this shattered the sense of normalcy. After the attack, Käthe's telephone rang with a call from the opera.

"Thanks to the English targeting civilian buildings, there will be no rehearsals or performances until further notice. The Staatsoper was bombed last night. We will provide more information as soon as we have it."

Käthe felt like she had fallen from a great height, knocking wind from her lungs. After processing this news, she sank onto the sofa and wept with grief. She took the news the same way as if her home had been bombed. Would she ever perform there again?

She felt thankful that Heidi was already at school by the time she got the call. She wouldn't have to explain her messy face. Her tears were not only the grief of losing a beloved building, and not only because of new uncertainty about her career, but also for a realization that no person or building was safe. This was not a military target; this was a cultural institution.

Randomness is terrifying.

By the next day, Käthe received another call that assuaged at least one of her fears—Hitler himself had ordered the opera to be rebuilt with construction to begin posthaste. He considered the opera essential for morale and wanted people to feel assured of a quick victory. Thus, Käthe would continue her training at a makeshift location until they could return to work in their new home. She wouldn't lose her job or her future.

After the opera was bombed, the air raids mostly stopped. The few that did happen dropped leaflets or small incendiaries. These were more of a disruption to the city than a genuine danger. People got back into their routines the best they could, embracing a sense of security for however long it would last.

Children continued to be evacuated from the city as part of the KLV program (*kinderlandverschickung*, which literally means sending children to the countryside), but Käthe wasn't about to send Heidi away, no matter how much her mother begged. Lucy was still around at times, which meant that having Heidi live at Oma's house was out of the question. Käthe's feelings were not only practical, she cherished having her daughter there. Besides, the bombings had calmed. They were fine.

CHAPTER FIVE

**MID-1941 THROUGH DECEMBER 1941:
PLAY TIME AND GRIEF**

AROUND THE TIME THAT HEDEL started dating Franz, and Käthe had met Werner, Käthe answered the door to the girl who lived on the top floor.

"I'm Ursula Bratfisch. Can your daughter play with me?"

"Does your mother know?"

"She's working."

"How old are you?"

"Seven."

Käthe let the girls get acquainted in the apartment and oversaw how they interacted. Heidi seemed older than five, and Ursula was a little young for her age, so the two got on fine. Ursula had fiery red hair, blue eyes, and pale, freckled skin. She wasn't a beautiful child, but she seemed bright and imaginative. Still, Käthe supervised because this was the first time for Heidi to have a playmate at home.

Ursula, who invited Heidi to call her Uschi, had rather unkempt hair and clothes. Käthe understood they were not well-off and tried not to judge unfairly. Uschi's mother worked as a cleaning lady for the apartment building, and her father was bedridden with cancer. Käthe found Uschi's mother to be a skittish person who seemed starstruck when she looked at Käthe. Frau Bratfisch only addressed Käthe in the most deferential way, like a domestic servant would to the lady of the house.

Frau Bratfisch had glasses, pulled her hair into a bun, and wore the title of cleaning lady more like an identity than an occupation. Certainly, Käthe hoped that Heidi would make friends with children of well-educated parents, but she also had compassion for the Bratfisch family. Uschi's father was terribly sick and could be heard moaning in pain. While everyone had their hands full with standing in ration lines and coping with restrictions, this family bore more than most.

The girls paged through Heidi's *Max and Moritz* book, and Heidi showed Uschi the radio. Uschi scanned the apartment like she had entered a palace. Heidi was thrilled to have made a friend, especially an older friend, and one who lived in the building.

After that, each day the two would call up or downstairs to each other, and Käthe began relying on Uschi to keep Heidi entertained when she had to run out. This friendship opened a new world for Heidi without long hours alone. Hers was now a world in which someone else joined in her games.

When Heidi got bored, she went into the stairwell and called, "Uschi, please come play!"

Uschi called down, "What will you give me?"

"Anything you want!"

"Can I play with the telephone?

"Sure!"

Uschi came over, and they made prank calls.

Sometimes they began playing indoors, but Uschi's father was in a lot of pain, so when they heard him moaning upstairs, they escaped outside. It was a terrible, helpless sound. The buildings on their block faced inward to a courtyard, giving the children a safe place to play.

Early one morning, Uschi and Heidi were playing in the courtyard, making a lot of noise, when their neighbor who lived upstairs, Frau Pohl, called down to them. "You, children. Why don't you make yourselves useful and fetch me some bread? I will pay for the errand."

Uschi asked, "How much?"

The woman named a price that would buy movie tickets. With that offer, the girls became business partners. The woman tossed down a piece of paper with the money for bread and her ration coupons folded inside.

"You get paid when you return," she hollered after them.

The girls were off, and along the way, they caught up to the most enormous dog either child had ever seen. It surely weighed more than Heidi and had a friendly face as he trotted along. He wore panniers like saddlebags to his sides, and he seemed to have a purpose. At first, the girls did not mean to follow him, but they stayed behind the animal out of curiosity. The dog made every turn they intended to make, and when they reached the baker, the dog sat at the front door and pawed at it, apparently waiting to be noticed.

The girls watched to see what would happen, and soon, the baker came to the door. He opened the dog's pouch, removed the ration coupons and money, and then placed one wrapped parcel of bread inside each pannier to balance the weight. The dog received his own chunk of bread as a reward.

Postponing their errand, they followed the dog to see where he would go. The dog retraced his steps, never getting distracted or stopping to sniff. When he returned to their street, he stopped in front of an apartment across from theirs. He then pawed a bell at the door, apparently installed for that purpose.

A woman opened the door to let the dog in and smiled when she saw the children with mouths agape.

Heidi curtsied and said, "Is this your dog?"

The woman seemed delighted at the girls' curiosity.

"His name is Barry, a St. Bernard. Barry is happiest when he has a job, and he fetches my bread every day."

"May we pet him?"

"Yes, you may, now that his work is done. He would like that."

Heidi was smitten. She had never witnessed anything so wonderous as this dog who could go to the baker alone.

"How does he know the way?"

The woman said, "His breed is trained to rescue people in the Alps."

Heidi marveled that this dog was doing the same work for which she and Uschi had been hired.

The woman seemed pleased by their affection and admiration. "Where do you live?"

The children pointed across the street.

"My name is Frau Schüller.[1] You may pet him any time after he returns with his job done. He misses children and mopes now that our son is in the Army."

Her voice caught, but she remembered herself and smoothed her apron.

Heidi did not want to leave Barry, but Uschi tugged at her. "Come on, we won't get paid if we dawdle."

When they returned with the bread, they hollered up, and Frau Pohl came down for the package and to pay the girls.

"What took you so long?"

Uschi lied easily. "The queue was long today."

Endless ration lines were the very reason the housewives keenly hired children to help. Buying any food item often required waiting, sometimes for hours to get a single

---

[1] This is her actual name, but a few details of her story have been combined with events that happened to another neighbor who was too minor a figure in this narrative to mention separately. All details are described here as Heidi remembered them, they just happened to two different—albeit real—people.

potato. Every family needed strategies. One scheme was for two women to hold each other's place. One might wait in the turnip line, while the other would stand for potatoes. In this way, two women could get *two* vegetables in the same amount of time. By hiring a child to go for bread, a resourceful mother could cobble together a meal.

That afternoon, Uschi took Heidi for their reward—a comedy playing at the Alexanderplatz theater called *Quax, Der Bruchpilot* (Quax, the Crash Pilot). Uschi taught Heidi the art of paying once and ducking into another theater after the first ended. When they finished the second movie, they emerged outside to dark skies.

It was 10 p.m. when Heidi came through the door, having skipped supper entirely. Käthe was pacing, frantic, and angry.

"Don't you ever make me worry about you like that again."

Heidi was contrite, and she curtsied to her mother. "I promise I will not do it again, Mútti."

Käthe caught herself from smiling at the curtsey, but she wasn't finished stewing. "I swear, child, if your father were here, I would send you to him."

Is that possible? Heidi wondered.

Käthe continued. "As punishment, you are not to play with Uschi until I say."

Heidi felt ashamed of doing the wrong thing and for worrying her mother.

But then, her thoughts shifted to a daydream of her father, which soothed her. Recently, she had begun imagining what it would be like to meet him. Tonight, one of these fantasies unspooled like a movie.

THE WAR IS OVER, AND HEIDI STANDS ON THE STREET UNDERNEATH ATLAS. SHE LOOKS UP TO SEE A SOLDIER WALKING TOWARD HER. WITHOUT

ANY INTRODUCTION, SHE KNOWS WHO HE IS BECAUSE HE IS THE BEST-LOOKING SOLDIER SHE HAS EVER SEEN. BESIDES, HE ALSO HAS HER DIMPLE.

HE SEES HER, AND HE KNOWS SHE IS HIS DAUGHTER RIGHT AWAY.

HE DROPS HIS BAG AND RUNS TOWARD HER. WHEN HE PICKS HER UP, HE SAYS, "YOU ARE EVEN PRETTIER THAN I IMAGINED. I TRIED TO GET HERE FOR YEARS, BUT THE ARMY KEPT ME AWAY. I WILL BE HERE FOR YOU FROM NOW ON."

Shortly after this, Käthe and Heidi learned that Uschi's father had died. Heidi felt sorry for her friend and wondered what it was like to have someone you love die. *At least she had known her father*, Heidi thought, with a touch of bitterness and jealousy.

Uschi did not come out of her apartment for a while. During that time, Heidi saw Käthe sewing two matching dresses, and she asked, "What are you making, Mútti?"

"A surprise."

When she finished, Käthe gave Heidi a dress and said, "The other is for Uschi. The two of you may play again. No child should have to lose their father so young."

Heidi cocked her head and said, "What about my father?"

Her mother said, "You can't miss someone you never knew."

But Heidi did miss her father. She missed knowing anything about him, and she was filled with questions. What was he like? Why had he never come to visit her? She resented her mother for not telling her more, and for not understanding why it mattered to hear about his good qualities. When Heidi felt her mother's bitterness toward him, she felt judged in the same ways. Was she not half her father?

In absence of facts, she made up her own to embellish the recurring daydream, adding variations with the heroic deeds he had done in the Army. Sometimes they went to the zoo or had tea together. Sometimes after her mother scolded her, she imagined living with him.

Still, Heidi did not ask her mother about her father. Käthe was softening but still could not speak about him kindly, and Heidi only wanted to hear nice things about him.

Käthe was a woman of big emotions, and her grief over a baby boy in a tiny coffin and the pain of betrayal would take a long time to heal. Maybe these wounds never would.

When Uschi was ready to come out and play, she showed Heidi her new ring with a sparkling blue gemstone. "My father gave it to me before he died. He picked it for the color of my eyes. It is to remind me of his love forever."

Heidi did not know what to say, and so she took her friend's hand and gripped it tightly.

Uschi never took the ring off from then on, and Heidi often caught her looking at it, glittering in the sun. The blue stone did look like Uschi's eyes.

Spring unfurled into summer, and they had several haunts around the city. They played tag around the Berolina statue with other children often joining in.

An older boy taunted them, "*Leck mich am arsch!*" Kiss my ass.

Right on cue, Uschi yelled back, "Run a little faster and you can kiss your own!"

One day while wearing their matching dresses, they went to the U-Bahn and waited until no passengers were around. Then, Uschi got on her hands and knees and crawled beneath the U-Bahn[2] turnstile, out of the ticket taker's view. Heidi followed.

As they rode to their stop, a passenger commented on their dresses.

"We're sisters," Heidi said.

The woman looked puzzled, "You don't look alike."

Uschi quipped, "She takes after our father."

At the pond, they stripped to their underwear and went swimming. The pond had logjams which gave them plenty to hang onto. Heidi had not yet been taught to swim above water, so she tadpoled under the surface from log to log.

Uschi said, "I have a song to teach you. You call out, 'What floats on the river Neisse?'"

So, Heidi called it out, matching the pitch perfectly.

Then Uschi called back the echo, "Scheisse!"

They roared with laughter.

The girls dried off and returned home, stealing their way onto the tram again. Heidi gazed out the window with contentment. *The best kind of day*, she thought.

Käthe sniffed at Heidi's hair. "Why do you smell like a swamp?"

Heidi shrugged. "We went wading."

---

[2] Heidi described the neighborhood, places, and walking distances in excellent detail during oral history interviews. Her remarkable memory was confirmed with a detailed map created by British intelligence during the war. That map—fortunately in English—showed the entire city with even its minor streets. Key buildings were identified on the back. This map was especially helpful for research because the Alexanderplatz neighborhood as Heidi remembered it no longer exists. The buildings and even the streets are all gone. The rubble was removed after the War, and the area built anew. With this map, Heidi located her street, the building where they lived, the U-Bahn station, and other landmarks. Her fingers traced the routes where she and Uschi had romped during those years. Source: Map. *Berlin: Allied Intelligence Map of Key Buildings, Reich Government, NSDAP, Police, Industrial, Utilities, Fire Service, Post Offices* (London: Photolithographed by War Office, 1945).

Käthe frowned. "Up to your hair? I will make an appointment for the bathhouse. You smell awful. You are sleeping on the sofa tonight."

Then, her mother repeated one of her favorite phrases of late, *If your father were here, I would give you to him.*

This time, Heidi thought to herself—but thought better than to say it aloud—*If he were here, I'd go.*

Instead, Heidi nodded, "Yes, Mútti." Heidi had long-ago accepted the futility of arguing with her mother.

Heidi decided they had better not go to the pond after that. If her mother learned the truth about how deep the water was where they had been swimming, she'd get a good hiding.

Käthe had reservations about Uschi, but she had seen gangs of rough children—especially the boys—and Heidi could have much worse friends.

■ ■ ■

On a clear and sunny June day, Heidi and her mother were preparing for a picnic with Werner. They packed lunch while listening to the radio, but the broadcast was interrupted by an official announcement. Käthe froze in place.

Germany had invaded Russia.

Käthe clasped her hands over her mouth to squelch a cry, "Oh, no. Oh *no*."

The news required Werner to cancel their plans and to report for an emergency meeting, so Käthe called Lizzie instead. In earlier times, Käthe would have invited Hedel for the outing, but although her sister still lived in the apartment, she usually wanted to spend time with her boyfriend.

So, Käthe, Heidi, Lizzie, and Wolfgang went to the park. Heidi half-heartedly entertained Wolfgang as Käthe and Lizzie talked. Heidi resented that her mother and Lizzie expected she would *want* to play with Wolfgang without ever asking her. Instead of being happy about it, she felt like they were pawning him off so they could enjoy themselves. Heidi liked playing with babies about as much as she enjoyed dolls, which was not very much. Wolfgang was two now, but she thought of him as a baby in the worst way. She glanced longingly at other children on the playground, but she decided to stay so she could hear the conversation.

Lizzie said, "I feel numb, like on the first day of the war, but not blindsided like we were then. Haven't we somehow known it would come to this?"

Käthe agreed. "When the soldiers all came home from France, I felt it could not be over so easy. I have been holding my breath for months."

Wolfgang kept running off the blanket. He was surprisingly fast given his off-balance teetering, so Heidi chased him down. He giggled. Now it was a game for him, which exasperated Heidi. "You stay right here!"

He had a mischievous look, eager to defy her.

Lizzie seemed unaware of the children as she gazed into the distance, and then whispered, "When Hitler said that Stalin was his new best man, I knew he was up to something."[3]

Käthe nodded, "It smelled like der mist."

Käthe said to Lizzie, "Now we will pay for the whims of these men."

Heidi looked up and saw that her mother's face had darkened with worry. It made Heidi feel afraid without fully understanding why. She let Wolfgang run away this time; Lizzie could chase after her son. Heidi was done playing baby games for the day.

---

3   Germany and Russia had longstanding grievances with each other, so their alliance was a surprising and tenuous one. It raised eyebrows at the time, and contemporaneous reports did not seem surprised when the relationship unraveled.

■ ■ ■

Despite people's fears following the announcement about Russia, there were no new bombings in their city for a while. It gave them a feeling of respite that the summer.

Heidi remained in kindergarten through the fall as she would not start school with the older children until after she turned six.

One day, Uschi asked Käthe if she could walk Heidi to and from school. This request came as a great relief to Käthe because it relieved her of having to pick Heidi up. That became their habit from then on.

In Heidi's kindergarten class, the teacher introduced a large map and asked if any children had a father, brother, or uncle serving in the war. Nearly every child had someone. Heidi felt lonesome when she pinned her father's name to the board. After that, one of the class's daily activities became to track locations of the German advance on the map.

That fall, Heidi noticed people wearing yellow stars on their clothing and asked her mother, who replied, "Don't stare, and don't ask in public."

Not long after that, Heidi saw that the people who lived in the ground-floor apartment wore a black upside-down triangle on their sleeves and again, she asked her mother.

"The people who live there are Romanis.[4] Their ancestors come from another place. Now they wear the triangle. Jews wear the yellow star. They are just different kinds of people."

Heidi had many questions, but they were interrupted by Uschi at the door.

"Can I take Heidi to the park?"

---

4   Heidi remembers everyone referring to the people downstairs as gypsies, which was a common term, but something of a slur even then.

Once outside, Heidi saw the mischievous look on Uschi's face and asked, "Where are we really going?"

The pair stole their way onto a train to a neighborhood with sprawling estates. Along the fence of one was a row of apple trees. The girls each picked two ripe apples and made a run for it.

Safely away from any denouncers,[5] their eyes rolled back in their heads at the juicy sweetness. Fresh fruit had practically become a memory, along with vanished marmalade, cookies, or candy.

Fall froze into winter as Heidi and Uschi romped through the first snowstorms and got into snowball fights. Then, one evening, Heidi returned home with her clothes wet all the way through to her skin.

Käthe wanted to help her change, but Heidi brushed her mother aside, "I learned to dress when I was three."

Käthe studied her child, and at dinner, Käthe put more generous portions of food before Heidi. The meal warmed Heidi from the inside out, and she felt fuller than she had ever felt in a long time. Heidi noticed her mother's eyes on her while she ate. "What's wrong, Mútti?"

Käthe shook her head.

But after dinner, she beckoned Heidi to the sofa, and Heidi noticed that her mother's eyes were moist.

Käthe paused a long while before speaking. "My darling, I have some very sad news. Your father has been killed in the war."

Heidi sat stunned and confused.

My father isn't dead. He is coming for me. He will hold me and protect me. We will see how alike we are.

"Get some rest, Heidi."

---

5   One tactic of the Nazis during the war was getting neighbors to spy and denounce (report) anyone who committed infractions against the state.

Käthe helped her to bed, and Heidi turned from her mother and curled into a ball. Käthe kissed the top of her head, pulled the quilt up, and decided to let her be.

The fantasy Heidi had rehearsed a hundred times began to roll like a movie, and tears sprung to her eyes. Those first tears were hot with rage at her mother.

She's lying. She has always hated my father. This is her fault. Why didn't she let me meet him?

But at the same time, Heidi did know that her mother would not lie about something like that. So she buried her face into the pillow and pounded fists into it.

She had long feared her mother dying, but she had recently taken comfort in thinking of her father. Now that was taken from her, too.

She ached for Oma, the village, and roasted apples. This thought made her cry harder.

While sitting on the sofa, tears rolled down Käthe's eyes, too. She had been angry for so long, and this news opened her wounds. There had been times when she wished him dead, but now she knew she hadn't really meant it. She only wanted things to be different, wanted absolution for all of them.

Now, Käthe only hoped for peace for him. She, too, wanted to rest from her burden of bitterness.

Hadn't she already shed enough tears over him? Here she was again. But somehow, these were not the bitter tears of before. These felt cleansing, like a saline wash that rinsed the wounds of her heart. This was healing like the sea.

She had blamed Alfred for everything, but new words came spilling out of her.

I am sorry. I am sorry. I am sorry.

She did not know why these words came. Sorry for what?

For everything. Because she had not been able to save their child or their marriage. For Heidi never knowing him.

I am sorry. I am sorry. I am sorry.
The words became a chant and a catharsis that she said until they stopped.
And then she was numb.
Käthe crept into the bedroom, now dark. Heidi lay on a wet pillow, her eyes red from shed tears. Käthe placed her palm across Heidi's back.
"Your father was a woodsman. You get your love of the forest from him."
"Really?"
Heidi turned toward her mother. Käthe drew Heidi's head into her lap, and Heidi nuzzled in. Then, Käthe began stroking her hair.
"He had twelve brothers and sisters. Can you imagine it? In the Czech countryside, the family had a business making furniture. He smelled of cedar, and he'd come home with wood shavings in his hair. He was happiest being outdoors with his dog. They'd go hunting, and I was always worried he would get in trouble for poaching. I remember once when his dog caught a wild hare. I didn't want to touch that thing, so I made him clean and skin it himself. He was never happy in the city. He wanted to go back and live around his family, but my dreams were here in Berlin. Something broke inside him when our baby boy got sick and died."
Heidi was sitting upright now, listening with rapt attention. She memorized the details and cached them into a safe place so she could retrieve them later.
Käthe's pale blue eyes were red with sorrow. "I am sorry he is gone. I wish you had a father."
With those words, Heidi clutched her mother's waist and forgave.
Käthe felt her daughter's warmth and added, "I believe he will watch over you. He and your little brother will be your guardian angels."

Hedel had been out with Franz, and when she came home, she glanced at her sister and braced herself for the worst, "What is it?"

Käthe steadied her voice before speaking. "I got *the letter* today," and handed it to her sister. There was no mistaking those words, *the letter*, which was shorthand that everyone understood those days.

Hedel exhaled, knowing she could breathe because the news hadn't been her worst fear—their parents were okay, Heidi was fine, and it wasn't an update about the war. Hedel read the brief, official notice that offered condolences that Alfred Machinek had been killed for the Führer and the fatherland on October 23, 1941.

Then, the sisters met each other's eyes, unsure what to say and with so many layers to navigate. Hedel's first instinct was to steer clear of Käthe, whose rage over Alfred could make her unpredictable. But Käthe was not volatile now. A drink had mellowed her sharp edges, and she was contemplative.

Hedel sat beside Käthe on the sofa and took her sister's hand.

Käthe said, "I can't believe he is gone, and he'll never know his daughter. I wanted him out, but not this. Now I wish it were different. I wish everything were different. Alfred, the war, everything. I hate that man."

Hedel looked surprised by this sudden shift in Käthe's mood, "Alfred?"

Käthe shook her head. "No, not Alfred. I mean, I did hate Alfred, but not now. I meant Hitler."

Hedel put her finger to her lips to shush her sister. "You can't say that."

"I know. But I am entitled to say it this once. Alfred shouldn't have ever been there. Heidi's father shouldn't be dead."

The two stayed that way for a long time until Hedel said, "We've seen death notices, but this is the first person I knew. The war is much too real today."

In the coming weeks, Heidi bounced back quickly, but sadness would descend upon her in unexpected moments when she played alone or if she spotted a soldier on the street. She often spoke to her father in private and hoped he could see and hear her.

Käthe noticed Heidi weeping sometimes when Heidi thought no one was looking, and it wrenched her heart. Käthe reminded herself that they were fortunate to at least know what happened to Alfred. They had the certainty of a death date and an answer. She saw the agony of women who received word that loved ones had gone missing. They didn't dare hope, and they didn't dare give up hope. Others simply stopped getting letters. The best-case scenario was that these men were still alive in a POW camp.

Käthe told the news to Werner who responded solemnly, "God bless him for his sacrifice for our country."

He studied Käthe for signs of how she was taking the news, but she did not reveal how she felt. It was too complicated to explain, even to herself. It would still take time for her to sort it out. Werner had let her be.

About two weeks later, when Käthe opened her yellow post box, her stomach knotted when she spotted an envelope. It was the kind of government-issued stationery that soldiers used to write home. Jumbled thoughts crowded her mind. Could it be a delayed letter from Alfred?

No, this is not his hand, she thought. Nevertheless, her legs gave way, and she slumped onto the floor to read it.

Dear Käthe,

I AM SORRY TO TELL YOU THAT ALFRED HAS BEEN KILLED ON THE RUSSIAN FRONT. I UNDERSTAND THAT FAMILIES NEED TO KNOW WHAT HAPPENED. WE WERE IN A FOXHOLE PLAYING CARDS, AND AFTER WINNING EVERYONE'S MONEY, HE LEFT OUR FOXHOLE TO FIND ANOTHER GAME. THE ENEMY SPOTTED HIM AND SHOT. HE WAS A GOOD FRIEND WHO FOUGHT BRAVELY. HE ALWAYS MADE ME LAUGH, AND I MISS HIM.[6]

That Christmas, Käthe, Heidi, and Hedel planned to take the train back to the village again. Werner went with them to the station. He had leave and would spend Christmas with his parents.

As soon as they settled in the train, Heidi asked her mother, "Why did Werner have your ring on his pinkie?"

"Oh, he admired it on me, so I let him borrow it."

At that, Hedel let out a little snort. "Nothing gets past this child."

As they rode, they saw how the train was packed with city people laden with household possessions. The passenger across from them had extra bags on his lap and held a rug rolled upright with his hands.

The man caught Käthe's glance and said, "I'll trade it with a farmer so I can feed my family a Christmas dinner."

Then he added, "I hear the pig stalls have Persian rugs these days. Farmers are getting rich from us starving in the city."

When they arrived, Heidi and Oma reveled in each other's arms again. On Christmas Eve, Heidi received a book of

---

[6] Heidi remembers her mother telling her about this letter, which described how her father died as indicated here. The letter did not survive the war, so Heidi does not know who sent it or the exact words.

Hans Christian Andersen fairy tales from her mother. Oma presented the girl with a lavish gift: a pair of used roller skates. The size adjusted and fastened over her shoes with a little key like one might use with a wind-up clock.

Käthe looked astounded, "How did you get these?"

Oma waved her daughter off. "Traded some goose fat and a few eggs for them."

During their visit, Oma did her best to fatten up her daughters and grandchild because she could see they needed it. She also hoped that eating well might persuade them to stay.

When the time came to leave, Oma pleaded with her daughter again to remain with them. "It's safer here. Nobody would bomb our village, and we have food. Think of Heidi *for once*."

That remark stung and Käthe shut her down, "How would I support myself? Mucking stalls? There are no jobs for a singer here, and I would never get my chance back. Besides, Hedel is in love, and nothing would keep her from Berlin now."

And so, the three returned to the city.

CHAPTER SIX

JANUARY 1942 THROUGH MID-1942: FORCED OUT

ONE MORNING IN EARLY 1942, Käthe and Heidi awoke to a ruckus on the street. They looked out the window to see the Romani family who lived downstairs being removed from their apartment. The grandmother, apparently refusing to leave, was being carried out while still seated on a chair, her arms folded in defiance and not making a sound. The other family members each carried one bag, and they looked frightened.

Käthe shooed Heidi away from the window.

"Where are those people going?"

"I hear they are being relocated to the east to make room for other people. After so many apartments got bombed, there are not homes for everyone. Some people must move."

"Will they make us move?"

"No. It's the Jews and Romanis who have to go."

"I don't understand."

"Neither do I, little mouse."

Käthe chewed on the thought. How could new people move in knowing someone else had been forced out? Some people must not care about the cost, or maybe they are gleeful at their good luck. Maybe they train themselves to banish such thoughts from their minds.

Rumor was constantly alight via Berlin's "mouth radio," as people called it—everything from speculation about food shipments, to the kinds of luxury items party officials enjoyed, to when the war would end.

But some things were not spoken of openly. Still, Käthe needed to know what would happen to her neighbors. So, when she went on a date with Werner, she pressed him on where people were being taken after evacuation.

"To the east. You know that."

"Der mist. Where are they really being sent?"

"I don't know."

"Yes, you do. You must."

"I know enough to know that I don't want to know. And neither do you."

Käthe would not relent, and he pushed back.

"I care for you and would have you safe. And while we are on the subject, it is conspicuous that you haven't joined the party. People are asking about your loyalties. I heard they plan to terminate anyone from the opera who isn't a member. If you get sacked, you'll be blacklisted. And that is a dangerous label to have."

"I can't join a party that makes people wear badges and that carries old women from their homes." She folded her arms and turned her head away from him.

"Look at me, Käthe, this isn't a game. You are a mother. There is a war going on, and I am not sure you realize how precarious the situation is. In times of war, you follow orders. You will not call attention to yourself. You will not call attention to me."

"Clearly, I am a liability to you."

He huffed. "Maybe you are."

She snapped, "I want my ring back."

That sent him reeling as though she had slapped him. Without a word, he slid the ring off his little finger and placed it in her palm.

"I'm sorry it is this way. I do not make the rules, but I do know what they are."

She looked out the window, hiding tears welling in her eyes. Werner let himself out of the apartment.

It was the last time they would speak. That conversation confirmed what Käthe had feared—everyone evacuated was in grave danger. Käthe grieved the breakup that night, and she went to bed early. Then, as had become her habit after a loss, she awoke the next day resolved to move forward. She phoned Lizzie with the news and invited her over that night.

Lizzie brought a bottle of schnapps to cheer her friend. She was happy to see Werner out of the picture, but she had enough tact to not agitate her friend's feelings. Instead, they laughed and told jokes while Heidi played with Wolfgang.

As the friends got drunk, their tongues loosened and Lizzie blurted, "You know who is to blame in all this?" Without saying the man's name aloud, she stood in Nazi salute to indicate that she meant Hitler.

Käthe nodded and said, "If I ever hear that he is dead, so help me God, I will dance on the table naked."

Heidi looked at her mother aghast and thought, *Oh please, stop! Nobody wants to see that, Mother!*

Heidi would never hear what became of Werner or if her mother ever learned. Heidi had grown fond of him, and his sudden absence was a loss that made her anxious about what might happen to other people she grew to love. Heidi had the dream again of her mother and the coffin, the dirt, and Heidi screaming. She frequently wet the bed after this, which was a deep embarrassment, but her mother always responded with compassion instead of blame.

■ ■ ■

One evening soon after, Käthe invited both Lizzie and her boyfriend over at a time when Hedel was at work. Käthe warned Heidi in advance. "Do not ask him about the star on his clothes. It is not polite."

"Mútti, I wouldn't do that."

Heidi was sent to bed while the grownups talked in tones too quiet for her to overhear. After that night, Lizzie's boyfriend stopped coming around.

In the coming days, Käthe had to make some decisions. She now realized that she had acted impulsively to break up with Werner. Gossip spread quickly in the theater; everyone knew who was dating whom and which couples were on the outs. Werner was indelibly connected with the authorities. What if the breakup left him in a retaliatory mood? She did not believe him to be a malicious person, but one could not be too careful.

Her situation was even more precarious than before, especially if she still refused to join the party.

At rehearsal, the manager tapped her shoulder and asked for a word. Her heart pounded. *What did he want?*

"Have you submitted your party application?"

"Not yet. I've had so much on my mind after my ex-husband was killed in battle."

"You can't make excuses forever."

He turned to leave, then paused. "You realize you owe your position here to the party, don't you?"

"How so?"

"The party engineered it. Your scholarship opened when they dismissed the Jewish swine. Then, talent scouts went to the hinterlands looking for blondes like you."

She tried not to react, but it felt like the wind had been kicked out of her.

"I did not know that," she whispered.

"You know it now. So show a little gratitude."

When she returned home, Käthe sent Heidi and Uschi out with movie money. Then she crawled back into bed and curled into a ball.

She buried her face into the pillow and screamed into it. Sobbing, she asked, "What am I to do, God? What can I do?"

I'm no better than people who moved into the apartment downstairs. I only have a place in the opera because others were kicked out."

When she quieted, she thought through her options, repeating, *What am I to do?*

About the time Heidi's movie would have finished, Käthe had worked out her answer. Werner predicted what would happen, and she sense it, too. If she didn't join the party, they would dismiss her. It now dawned on her that she must leave of her own accord before they sacked her.

Now, a new wave of tears came. This was one of the three hardest moments of Käthe's life, the first being when she saw her baby's body in a tiny coffin. That had felt unbearable, and so was this. The next crushing experience was learning her husband and sister had betrayed her.

Each of these experiences meant the loss of her future, sadness for what might have been, and anger for what should have been. Each time, a dream was taken from her.

The unfairness stung hot. She was learning how deeply cruel this life could be. She now knew that she had benefitted from someone else. Their loss had made her scholarship possible. Her opportunity had not been created; it had been taken from someone else.

It wounded her to think that when she had been showered with good fortune, she had pridefully attributed it to her talent and hard work. Now she saw the truth—her place had come at another's expense.

Now it was being ripped from her grasp, too. So maybe this blow wasn't unfair after all. Maybe it was just her turn to pay. *Maybe it was penance.*

But what would she tell people if she left? She had been introduced as a "rising star." What was she now? Nothing. She didn't know if she could stomach people's judgment. What would they think of her to have thrown away such a chance? On whose faces would she read schadenfreude? Their smugness would make her fall from the sky even more painful.

She had the bitter thought that she might be better off mucking stalls in the countryside after all.

Her pride was in shreds, but she would salvage her dignity by doing what she knew she must of her own accord. She wouldn't wait to be dismissed.

In the coming days, feelings of bitterness toughened into resolve, and she worked on a plan. But first, she had to figure out a way to support herself. Quickly.

She confided in her sister how sad she felt at the breakup and how she feared for her job. She had been acting like she didn't care, but her world was crumbling. She told Hedel that she knew she would be blacklisted at the opera if she didn't join the party, and she would have to leave.

When Hedel saw how much her sister was hurting, she said, "You are the most determined person I know. You will land on your feet when the war ends. All this is temporary until then."

Then Hedel bit her lip, unsure how to frame what she had to offer.

"I know where you can get hired."

Käthe stopped her. "I know what you are going to say. I don't think I can work in a factory."

Hedel bristled. "You are too good to work like the rest of us? To mingle among peasants?"

"I didn't mean it like that. I am sorry. I will think about it."

And Käthe did think about it. She mulled it over until realizing that she had little choice. She must act quickly, or else she might be unable to act at all.

She swallowed her pride, applied at the factory, and they hired her on the spot.

Hedel congratulated her sister, but Käthe couldn't muster enthusiasm for getting a new job—even though it paid better than the stipend she received from the opera. Instead, it felt like she had been sentenced. Would she ever get the chance to sing on such a stage again? How long must she put her dreams on hold?

It's just until the war ends, she told herself.

Despite her fears and heartbreak, she put in her notice, giving the premature excuse that her sister was getting married, and she now lacked childcare during the opera's evening performances when Heidi was not in school.

On the first morning of her new position, Käthe walked with leaden feet to the factory. She found the assembly work numbingly tedious, surrounded by the dull gossip of small-minded people. To pass the time, she daydreamed of the war ending and getting a fresh start as a singer somewhere else.

In the coming weeks, a realization dawned on her that she was working to help a cause she despised more with every passing day. *How could she have stooped to this?*

Meanwhile, Lizzie had other ideas for her friend. Her boyfriend had taken the plunge into the abyss, becoming a human U-boat by removing the star and diving under.[1] In doing so, the couple had become introduced to Berlin's underground, opening their eyes to a network of helpers, subversives, and black-market dealers.

It wasn't entirely a surprise to them—in those days, everyone had become a petty criminal in buying or selling illicit goods. It didn't matter who you were—the wife of a party official with connections to the best black-market fare or a housewife in the ghetto looking for an extra potato. One simply couldn't get by on what was available through

---

[1] The phrase "taking the plunge" was used by Jewish people who opted out of society by removing the star. For a time, some tried to blend in, some tried to leave Germany, and a few were helped to obtain non-Jewish identities and live in plain sight. All would need the help of others to survive.

the ration system. That reality desensitized everyone to the shades of gray. Still, widespread participation in the black market did not fully neutralize the risk.

It also happened that Alexanderplatz was a hotbed of black-market activity. Especially in that neighborhood, it seemed that everyone was guilty in some form, making denouncement a lower risk. It was also easier to get connected and to go unnoticed. Everyone had their sources for things, and everyone learned to play in reciprocity.

Lizzie needed favors for her boyfriend, and they needed connections she could trust. Likewise, her network was recruiting able bodies to join the black-market economy.

They first enticed Käthe with an almost irresistible offer: a brick of real coffee that she could repackage and sell. Her take was to skim a portion for herself as profit. When she had distributed this, she'd receive more foodstuffs that would supplement her factory wages. She carried out this assignment while Hedel was at work. It was easy enough, and it felt good to do something subversive. She quickly received new responsibilities.

Then, just as Käthe was about to lose her mind in boredom in the factory job, Hedel came home with joyful news.

"Franz got approved to go home. We will be on the next train and can get married in his church."

Käthe was thrilled for her sister and relieved for her own sake. Now, she wouldn't have to be so careful to hide her activities in the apartment. She could quit her job as soon as she had built up some savings to cover the rent. She now had a goal to work toward.

The sisters were soon kissing one another goodbye. Käthe presented Hedel with a wool suit of her own that she had been secretly altering to Hedel's size, anticipating this day. Its elegant simplicity would do nicely for Hedel's wedding.

They embraced, and then Hedel was gone.

CHAPTER SEVEN

MID-1942 THROUGH DECEMBER 1942: UNDERGROUND AND MOVED AROUND

A FIRST ORDER OF BUSINESS was to conserve resources any way possible now that she wouldn't have Hedel helping to pay the rent. So she moved a wardrobe in front of Hedel's door and put their bed into the living room. It would save heat if they lived in just one room.

With Hedel gone, Käthe took on more assignments, which empowered her. It felt like her illicit activities were a counterbalance to her factory work. It turned out she had a knack for it, too. Käthe's natural charm and resourcefulness made her an asset. She was careful, but she did allow Heidi to help.

Sometimes they got wine and would uncork each one, pour a little from each bottle into a new one, water all of them down, then recork them. Another premium commodity was tobacco mailed in hollowed-out books. Heidi learned to roll cigarettes, which her mother could sell for about five reichsmarks a piece. That should have been good money, but currency had less value all the time. She fared better when she traded them directly for other items that were worth more to people. The street value of goods meant that working in trade through the underground was quickly becoming more profitable than her factory job.

After learning to roll cigarettes, Heidi and Uschi figured out on their own that they could pick up cigarette butts at Alexanderplatz, then combine all the leftover tobacco and roll secondhand cigarettes for sale. These fetched less than the premium ones her mother offered, but it was still movie money.

With their cigarette proceeds one afternoon, Heidi and Uschi went to a romance movie called *Zwei in Einer Großen Stadt (Two in a Big City, 1942)*. In one scene, the lead couple went to the Strandbad Wannsee, a Berlin beach where Hitler brought in gorgeous sand from the Baltic Sea. The girls salivated as the couple got ice cream cones. However, when the heroine got angry with her love, she stuck her cone into the sand and ran away. Her lover then put his ice cream into the sand and ran after her. Heidi and Uschi couldn't stop talking about that scene. The image of two melting and wasted ice cream cones would stay with Heidi for a lifetime.

One day, the two girls were home alone, and they spotted a group of work camp laborers repairing the street below. Uschi talked Heidi into retrieving some of her mother's cigarette inventory, which they threw down and snickered as the men scramble like chickens. That was great fun for a minute. Käthe never missed the cigarettes, or they would have been in big trouble.

Another item they dealt in was coffee. To pick it up, they would go to a Swiss woman's shop that had previously sold the finest chocolate and coffee. Although the shelves were now bare, the moment they walked in, Heidi was struck by the smell of real coffee, a scent she always liked. The proprietor was a short Swiss woman no taller than Heidi, who had bleached-blonde hair and a thick French accent when she spoke to Heidi. Heidi learned to love those visits because the woman always gave her some of whatever sweets she had on hand. When Käthe and the woman conversed, Käthe spoke French.

The way coffee got into the country was through a network of Swiss immigrants. One would board a train in Switzerland with bricks of real coffee in a suitcase, the good stuff. After crossing into the German side, the smuggler would step between train cars and toss the coffee into a farmer's field. Then, the next contact would find the bricks using a sniffing dog that was trained for the job. The coffee then made its way from the farmer's field into Käthe's apartment. In the apartment, Heidi helped by opening each brick, scratching the coffee out with a fork, and dividing it into portions that would make a single pot of coffee. The value of a pot of coffee had become almost unimaginable by then. Heidi breathed in the scent of it, embedding the memory deep within her.[1]

By now, Käthe had a growing and gnawing unease about Heidi being around her illicit activities, and now her daughter's friend was seeing things, too. Sooner or later, one of them might let something slip. She agonized over this problem until, one day, Lizzie presented a solution.

"I am sending Wolfgang to my parents' villa in the countryside as part of the KLV program. My parents are wealthy, and there is plenty of food there. Heidi would be welcome to go, too. She could help with Wolfgang, which would work out for everyone. Heidi would have run of the grounds. She'll be safer there, and who knows what kind of trouble she gets in all day in the city."

Käthe agonized over the decision, but Lizzie talked her into it. She knew their black-market dealing put the children in danger.

When Käthe told Heidi of the decision, Heidi begged her mother to let her stay in the city or send her to Oma.

---

[1] Some of Heidi's memories of her mother smuggling coffee were from during the war, and some were from after, related to smuggling it into the communist sector of Berlin. It was difficult to untangle which memory fragments were from which timeframe.

But when Käthe said, "Enough!" she meant it. Heidi sulked in private, feeling she was being cast aside. She believed she could help her mother in the city, or at least not be any trouble.

Before long, Heidi and Wolfgang had placards around their necks stating their destination in occupied Poland. They boarded at Anhalter station. Heidi's lips quivered while holding little Wolfgang's chubby hand. She willed herself to not cry, but she was losing the battle. The feelings she had the first night she was left in The Mother Eva House welled up within her, reopening that wound fresh.

"We need you to be a big girl and help Wolfgang. Can you do that?" Heidi resented the request. Who would help her?

It was a chilly day, and Heidi felt abandoned again. She was just a month short of six years old, and Wolfgang was not quite three—the same age Heidi had been when she went to The Mother Eva House. She knew it was not his fault, and she felt a pang of compassion for what he was about to go through, but she also couldn't help herself from blaming him a little. She believed she wouldn't be sent away if he were not in the picture.

Käthe placed Heidi into the care of a train worker who was well-practiced in the exercise, and Käthe promised Heidi, "I will visit in June, and we will decide what to do then."

Heidi clutched the big doll Oma had given her, but its cold porcelain face was not of the living world. Whenever a grownup spotted it, they fawned over such a beautiful doll, but to Heidi, it was a dead thing with glass eyes and limbs that bent at unnatural angles. They placed it into her arms, expecting it to be of comfort, so she took it. But it had the opposite effect; it was another reminder of the last time she had been left behind at The Mother Eva House and Oma visited but did not take her home.

On the train, she pined for the scent of her mother or the folds of Oma's lap. She wanted a living friend in Uschi, not a doll. She wanted playmates, not a brat to look after.

It was the time of winter when once-fresh snow had turned a dingy gray, and coal smoke made the air thick. The world seemed as gray and bleak as Heidi's aching little heart. Wolfgang napped, and her mind turned to thoughts of her father. Tears rolled down her cheeks and she pressed her forehead to the chilled window.

At last, the train slowed toward their station, and a female attendant sought Heidi, then guided the two children onto the platform. There were very few people there, and a woman approached.

"I'm Frau Lupinski," the woman said in German, heavily accented with Polish.

Heidi curtsied and gave her hand as she had been taught. "How do you do."

"You look small for seven."

Heidi corrected her. "I'm five, almost six."

"Come along then." She picked up Wolfgang and Heidi's suitcase. Heidi managed the doll.

Frau Lupinski clucked. "I thought you were seven."

Heidi bristled. "I won't be any trouble. I learned to do things for myself at The Mother Eva House."

"We shall see."

The woman's adult son—Lizzie's brother—drove their car into the countryside and eventually pulled onto a tree-lined drive.

A stone villa dominated the property. Heidi had hoped for the warmth of The Mother Eva House, but this place seemed frozen, and winter dusk cast long shadows over it. The windows were shuttered, and Heidi did not see anyone outside.

Behind the villa lay a fenced area, probably a kitchen garden blanketed in snow.

The entire estate had seen better days.

Heidi thought of how The Mother Eva House felt inviting, as though welcoming all visitors to come inside to rest from their cares. This place would scare them away.

They entered through heavy wooden doors with iron hinges. One thing changed Heidi's mood right away—the smell of food cooking wafted over her and made her drool.

"I expect you're hungry. I put on a rabbit stew."

Heidi nodded.

"Wash up in the basin here."

As Heidi washed, she heard the door open and heavy boots on the stone floor. Lizzie's father was returning from his work. He had become a ragged laborer, no longer seeming like the blue-blood patriarch of a grand house.

Everyone in that part of Poland had fallen on hard times.

They did not take their meal in the dining hall; instead, they ate in the warm cook kitchen on a heavy table where servants used to take their meals.

Frau Lupinski was out of practice managing mealtime with a young child, and they turned their attention to their grandson. That suited Heidi. She did not feel like talking, and the stew tasted delicious, served with crusty bread like the kind Oma made.

That thought gave Heidi a pang, and she wished again that she had been sent to Oma.

The home had never been fitted with electric lights, so Frau Lupinski retrieved her carbide lamp, which cast spooky shadows on the walls.

She led Heidi to the room of long-since-grown children.

"This was the nursery. The toys will keep you entertained. Do you need help getting ready for bed?"

Heidi shook her head, "No."

"I'll show you the grounds tomorrow."

They would make up a bed for Wolfgang in their room.

Although it was not late, it seemed so. Heidi was worn out, so she crawled into bed. There was no fire in the fireplace nor other heat in her room, but the blankets warmed her quickly. It was a comfortable featherbed like the ones at Oma's house, and she burrowed deep under the covers. Soon she was asleep.

When Frau Lupinski woke Heidi for breakfast, Heidi could see their breath. She dressed quickly and was not disappointed when she entered the kitchen to find it smelling of eggs. Heidi devoured her soft-boiled egg, a hard roll, and a cup of milk.

Over breakfast, she was given strict instructions to close every door. They only had enough coal to heat the kitchen and study, and only for part of the day. Beyond that, she'd have to wear her coat and keep moving.

Heidi inquired, "Do you have any animals?"

"A milk cow, rabbits, geese, chickens, and pigs. The geese are mean, but you can play with the rabbits. When the piglets are born in the spring, you can play with them. You will feed the chickens and collect eggs each day."

"I would like that."

Heidi's heart soared when she saw the bunnies in their cages. "May I play with them now?"

Frau Lupinski shrugged and left her with the bunnies. "We don't have enough food for lunch these days, so you may come in for a cup of milk at noon. Dinner will be at seven."

Heidi ventured out to explore the grounds for a little while, but she spent most of that first day playing with the rabbits.

A Child In Berlin

There was no playschool,[2] and no other children lived nearby. It was just the old man and woman. Heidi spent her time helping look after Wolfgang and the animals, naming each one and telling herself stories about them. The days felt long, but Heidi had been learning to entertain herself since birth. Now she was finding ways to keep Wolfgang out of trouble.

Sometimes when Wolfgang napped, she shrank into a corner, making herself all but invisible, and she studied Frau Lupinski. This woman was not like Oma. There was something odd about how her clothes had once been fine but were now dingy and threadbare. She seemed poorer than Oma even though she had such a large house filled with paintings and antiques.

Heidi never saw Frau Lupinski do laundry or clean in the same ways that Oma did. Oma and Käthe were strict in doing every task a certain way, and they were always explaining to Heidi the proper way and why it was so. But this woman's movements seemed unsteady, like she was doing that thing for the first time.

Heidi could not know how the old couple strained under the weight of German occupation designed to break them by extracting all that could be taken. Unable to manage their responsibilities with so little, Frau Lupinski had to let much of her refinement go. Now she seemed coarse for being exhausted and falling so far from her upbringing.

Sometimes, the ache of loneliness washed over Heidi with such a heaviness that she could hardly move. She'd go into her room and hug her bony knees. If anyone had noticed her, she would have seemed so tiny at those times. But no one ever did.

---

2 The war children of Berlin who were not sent to Hitler Youth programs lost years of education during all the upheavals they experienced. They were shuttled from place to place, and the regular school system largely collapsed.

On March 12, Heidi did not realize that her birthday had come until the woman handed her a brown paper package. Heidi ripped into it and found a new dress sewn by her mother. She pressed it to her nose, hoping for the scent of her mother, but it carried none. Still, she was glad for something pretty to wear.

For dinner that night, the old woman made almond cookies as her gift to Heidi. Heidi was grateful for the cookies, but her birthday was not a happy occasion.

The next day, while Heidi was playing with the bunnies, the old woman entered the stone barn and opened a latch.

Heidi wondered what she was doing as she roughly retrieved one of the rabbits by its feet.

Without acknowledging Heidi, she walked to the stone wall and swung the rabbit with a giant motion, bashing its head. It wriggled, and so she hit it against the wall again.

Heidi shrieked.

The woman bristled, "How do you think we eat?"

Heidi wanted to be sick. She knew where food came from and that rabbits were not pets, but it was such a violent act that she couldn't look at the woman for days. How could she be so brutal, without emotion for the animal? She didn't realize that never in this woman's life had someone like Oma taught her how to do laundry, efficiently clean, or humanely slaughter an animal. She had been reared with refinement, not for surviving hard times. The adults in Heidi's life were trained to be capable and self-reliant. They loved her. Heidi had never been around anything else, and she did not have language to put words to what was wrong. She just sensed that the villa was broken, the people felt broken, and that she shouldn't be there. The ache of not belonging with these people was a greater pang than hunger had ever been.

When Heidi entered the villa that night, the smell of rabbit stew nauseated her. She could not erase the image from her mind.

Another month passed, and to Heidi's great amusement, the piglets were born just as the weather turned warm. Soon they would come running when Heidi entered the barn. They ran around at her feet, squealing and playing. Heidi was smitten with love for them, nuzzling them like they were her babies.

The animals were the only bright spot for her during the otherwise gray time she lived there. Her feelings about it would forever be sodden, like a newspaper left out in the rain. Neglect had made that part of her story clump together, and the sting of abandonment kept her from ever trying pull the pages apart. Some memories are better left to decompose.

Then one day, as honeybees buzzed in the flowering orchard, Käthe arrived. It was early May, a month earlier than she said she would come. When Käthe entered the grounds, she shuddered.

This was not what Lizzie had described, a house of lively parties and privilege. Käthe wondered how long it had been since Lizzie had visited her parents, and she felt a chill of realization at how quickly society could crumble.

At their reunion, Käthe saw Heidi's dull complexion, and her heart broke. Heidi hadn't lost weight, but her color was drained, as though Heidi had retreated into herself.

Käthe had come early because she sensed that all was not well. She had already decided to bring Heidi home because she had been unsuccessful in convincing herself that sending Heidi there had been for the best. She had regretted the decision almost immediately, especially because there had been no bombings in quite a while.

Seeing her now gave Käthe a sense of guilt. It was a painful realization that nobody could look after her daughter like she would.

"I am taking you home, my treasure."

"When?"

"Right now."

Heidi buried her head into her mother's chest.

That was when Käthe gasped and pulled an arm's length away from her daughter.

"What's wrong, Mútti?"

"Did you know you have lice?"

Heidi nodded yes. She had been scratching like mad and would shake lice onto a chalkboard slate, then crunch them dead with the flat side of her fingernail. It was the only way to be rid of them.

"I will fix this when we get back to Berlin. But we need to keep some distance for now, or else I'll get them too."

When they got home to Berlin, Käthe used her good sewing scissors to cut off Heidi's beautiful hair. Then she treated her scalp with kerosene to kill the lice. It burned terribly on the wounds where Heidi had been scratching, and she cried. Käthe's eyes welled up, too.

"Stop, Mútti, it burns!"

But Käthe did what had to be done, and the treatment worked.

Käthe acquired a hairpiece with a hat that Heidi could wear to make it look like she had hair until it grew back in. She wasn't the only child to suffer from lice, and mothers had ways of making do.

Eager for playtime, Heidi reconnected with Uschi right away. Their favorite activities were movies whenever they had money and roller skating when they did not. Since Heidi's skates gave no ankle support, she twisted her ankles and had skinned knees, but bruises and scrapes never stopped her.

■ ■ ■

One day, Frau Pohl, the neighbor upstairs, came to the door with puffy eyes. She and Käthe had become friends, sometimes babysitting each other's children, and helping each other with the ration queues.

Käthe welcomed her inside as she would with any friend, for Käthe always had a listening ear.

On the sofa, Frau Pohl wrung her hands like she was giving them a thorough washing.

"You know my boy, the slow one? I took him to the doctor. They said I should leave him overnight for treatment. The sweet boy has rarely been out of my sight, so I didn't want to, but I hoped they could help him."

Käthe nodded. "I'm sure you did the right thing."

But the woman shook her head. "I went today to bring him home, and they said he wasn't feeling well. I wasn't allowed in, not to see my own child!"

Käthe looked alarmed. "When can you return?"

"Tomorrow. Pray for my boy. I have a premonition."

Käthe took the woman's hand. "I will. I am sure your son will be fine."

The next day, the woman came again. "I have a terrible feeling. He was lying there like a sack of flour. His eyes looked straight ahead like a glass doll, and he was drooling."

"Did they say what his illness was?"

"That's just it. He wasn't sick when I took him. I only wanted to check his hearing."

"Maybe it came on suddenly."

The woman held up her hand, panting with rage. "I saw something else. All the children in that ward were handicapped. And all the children had the same look. It sounds crazy, but what if they are *making* those children sick? They wouldn't let me bring him home. My poor, poor boy."

Käthe took Frau Pohl's hand, "I am sure there is a good explanation."

Käthe wanted to believe that, but she had already seen too much—Lizzie's boyfriend and his people, then what she learned about the opera, and Romanis marched from the building.

But children?

Frau Pohl was as Arian as anyone. Would they really harm a child because he was slow? Käthe shuddered.

Frau Pohl returned after a few days and collapsed at the threshold, sobbing.

Käthe felt panic in her gut. *What happened?*

"He is gone. The schweinehunds killed my son. I would have gladly taken care of him the rest of his life, but they took him from me." Frau Pohl's whole body shook with grief and rage. "How could they? Only monsters kill children."

Käthe felt smacked with physical shock; she had no words. She could never have believed it before, but now she had to.

The two women did not realize that Heidi was eavesdropping on every word and trying to make sense of what she heard. Could it be true? Either the boy's mother was telling a wicked lie, or doctors had killed a little boy. Heidi did not know how to process either possibility. That boy had been the sweetest child. Yes, he was a different kind of boy, but he always seemed to have a smile on his face, and he'd extend his arms for affection from Heidi whenever they passed. She had not quite known what to think of him, so she had just accepted the explanation that he was "slow but loving." It felt like the room was spinning, and every time she tried to close her eyes, the image of the little boy's face came to her mind. The very idea of what Frau Pohl had said chilled her insides.

When Käthe found Heidi sullen in her room, Heidi admitted that she had overheard, and that it had upset her.

Käthe tried to comfort her child, but what could she say? Honesty was all she could muster. She must teach Heidi to be wary.

"We cannot trust everyone, but do not fill your head with the cares of grownups. You will have plenty of time to be an adult later."

Heidi replied, "I am never going to the doctor."

■ ■ ■

There had only been one bombing throughout 1942, but by fall, everyone was sullen when they spoke of the Battle of Stalingrad. Letters that made it home were censored, so people in Berlin could only surmise how bad it was by counting the men they personally knew who were killed. From that tally, they understood it was a bloodbath.

One day, Frau Schüller (the neighbor with the bread-delivering St. Bernard) was bursting with joy when her son returned home from the Army with an injury. He was laid up but alive!

She invited Heidi over. "My son will read to you. It will pass the time and be good for his spirits."

Heidi loved to be read to, and so she was glad for the invitation. He motioned her to a chair by the sofa, and she tried not to stare at his cast.

He read Heidi a story about a hunchback boy with a tender soul. People would point and laugh at him. He did not fight with them. He spent his time alone in the woods, where he made friends with the animals. One day, the boy fell ill and died, and the only person who came to his funeral was his mother. But then she saw creatures at the edge of the forest forming a ring around the graveside—animals of all kinds. High in the treetops, the birds sang him a song.

As Heidi listened to the story, tears welled up in her eyes. She usually thought of her father when she heard sad tales, but this time she remembered the little boy with the round face who had always been so friendly. She couldn't keep the image from coming to her mind at various times, imagining this poor little boy taken from his mother, and how he had glassy eyes like the doll she never liked.

Heidi was not afraid of ghosts or demons. She felt safe in the dark, not frightened like other children might be. But this image of the little boy in the hospital haunted her imagination, coming into mind when she wanted to think happy thoughts.

The man stopped reading when he noticed Heidi crying and said, "Wait, there is more to this tale."

He turned the page.

When the hunchback boy went to heaven, he admired the angels with their outstretched wings. One angel noticed his hunch and gathered the others. The boy felt ashamed like he had been in life. He braced himself, waiting for others to point at him. He wanted to hide.

Then, an angel with the broadest wings asked the boy, "My child, don't you know what your hunch is?"

The angel placed her hand upon his back, and when she did, a magnificent pair of wings sprouted from it.

"You were born with an angel's spirit, and these wings have been forming in your hunch for your whole life. An angel takes a long time to get wings, but yours got an early start. They have been growing since your birth as a mortal."

By the end of the book, Heidi was so spellbound that she had moved next to the soldier, leaning her head on his shoulder.

■ ■ ■

A few days later, Käthe noticed she had picked up crabs in her underarm hair. How on earth could she have gotten crabs? She was very clean and hadn't been close to anyone since Werner.

Soon after, she noticed that Heidi's eyes were red and itchy, as though she had an infection. There was something that looked crusty on her eyelid, and when Käthe scratched at it, the crust moved. She reflexively jerked her hand back. Crabs!

Since Käthe and Heidi slept in the same bed, they both had crabs. It was just that crabs attach to hair, and the only real hair on Heidi's body was her eyelashes, so that is where they were found.

Now they just had to solve the mystery of how crabs had been brought into the house. A few days later, Käthe stood chatting in the ration line with Frau Schüller.

Käthe thanked the woman for her kindness toward Heidi and said, "I trust your son is recovering. But not *too quickly*, of course."

The woman said, "He is doing better each day."

Then Frau Schüller lowered her voice to a gossiping tone.

"Except imagine my horror when I realized that he brought back crabs from abroad."

Käthe made light of it, "Didn't all the soldiers? It's a gift from France, you know. Champagne and crabs to go with it."

The two women laughed. Then, the realization dawned on Käthe. Heidi had nestled in at story time, and crabs had jumped from the man's hair to Heidi's eyelashes, and then from Heidi to Käthe. What must they endure next?

Heidi looked forward to starting first grade that fall, having graduated from kindergarten and into regular school with the big kids. She walked to school wearing a leather backpack while holding hands with Uschi.

The children sat at little desks that each had a chalk slate and a wet sea sponge to wipe it clean. Each desk also had an inkwell built into the front. When girls with long braids sat in front of boys, the boy sometimes dipped the braid tips into the inkwell. The boys would be disciplined for this, but it must have been worth it, because this was a common prank. Heidi was only free from this indignity because her hair was still just stubble. She continued to wear her hairpiece with bob-length curls.

Heidi learned her ABCs and numbers quickly but enjoyed art projects best. Drawing came easily to her.

On Saturdays, she loved attending a half day for athletics. She played sports, and Heidi discovered she was stronger than other children. She could pull herself up on the monkey bars and throw a ball hard.

On Sundays, Käthe often dropped Heidi off at the Catholic church they sometimes attended so Heidi could go to a children's service. This church was more modest than the one in Oma's village because Berlin was mainly Protestant, and the neighborhood church reflected this.

Heidi liked going. It felt familiar, reminded her of Oma, and Heidi liked the idea of being in the presence of God. While Heidi's mother was not especially religious, she taught the girl to live by the golden rule saying, "How would you like it if someone did that to you?" Käthe would attend on occasion, but most often sent Heidi on her own.

Now that some time had passed since the break-up with Werner, Käthe had begun dating other men, but she did not bring any of them home to meet Heidi.

One evening, however, Käthe invited a dignified Swiss man named Richard Sauerbrey to the apartment for dinner. He brought a brick of coffee and said, "For you, not for selling."

Käthe brought it to her nose and drew in a long breath, savoring the extravagance of such a present.

Richard wore perfectly pressed clothes and seemed a little standoffish toward Heidi at first, and Heidi instantly judged him. *So stuck up*, she thought.

Käthe had set the table with her best dishes and linens, and Richard sat with the same sort of perfect posture as Käthe's. He enjoyed the meal with enthusiasm, complimenting the cook. But Heidi—always hungry—gawked at him while he ate. Käthe shot her a look that asked without words, *What is your problem?*

Heidi blurted out, "He's eating all our food."

Richard's straight posture did not change, but at Heidi's words, he set down his fork, dabbed the corners of his mouth with a napkin, and announced, "Thank you. I've had quite enough."

He did not touch another bite, leaving his plate half uneaten, and Heidi was sent away from the table for being rude.

After the evening, Käthe asked, "What did you think of him?"

"He walks with his nose in the air."

Käthe was incensed, "Don't ever say that. I like him."

Heidi asked, "Why?"

"He comes from a prominent family and went to the best schools. He speaks languages and is one of the most intelligent people I've ever met. Richard can add long columns of numbers in his head. He's a marvel."

Heidi held her tongue after that.

Soon after, Käthe sat Heidi on the sofa and said, "I have something to tell you."

Heidi did not like the sound of her mother's tone.

"Richard and I are getting married."

"Will he live with us?"

"No. He has already been conscripted into the Army and will leave soon."

"Do I have to call him dad?"

"Not if you don't want to."

"Are you in love?"

"That's none of your business. But yes. In a way."

"When will it be?"

"We don't have much time. Tomorrow. Afterward, we will all go out for a nice dinner."

With the promise of a big restaurant meal and the assurance that she would not have to put up with Richard in their house, Heidi was pacified.

It was November, so Käthe got Heidi ready in her prettiest dress and a button-up coat. She also wore a hat with the hairpiece since hers had not grown in yet. They all went to the courthouse for a perfunctory marriage. Lizzie was there, but no other friends.

In those days, photographers in certain parts of town waited at kiosks for customers. You could walk up and pay them to take a picture of you. And so, Richard hired one to snap a photo of the three of them, hand-in-hand on the street, all smiles. Käthe beamed at Richard with adoration.

After the wedding, they walked along the cobblestone to their favorite fish restaurant at Alexanderplatz.

That night and for the following night, Heidi stayed with Frau Pohl, her daughter, and the elderly mother upstairs.

After the honeymoon, Richard went away to a special training program. His paychecks were sent home to Käthe like Heidi's father's had been. Käthe continued to receive shipments from Switzerland on his behalf, including coffee and tobacco in hollowed-out books. The wedding did not affect their lives; Heidi and Käthe continued as though nothing had changed.[3]

---

3   It is impossible to know how Käthe really felt about Richard at the time of their wedding. Heidi recalls that her mother was impressed by him: his education, intelligence, blue-blood family in Switzerland, good manners, and dress. He was a nice-looking man. They did not know each other all that well, but Käthe was a woman of big emotions, and it isn't difficult to imagine her falling for someone quickly especially since she was still bouncing back from Werner. Were they in love? Or was it a more of business arrangement at first? It was not uncommon for people to marry hastily before the men went to war because a pension would be sent to the widow in the event of their death. We do know that Heidi was not very happy about the idea of it, but the marriage had little impact on her life at that time. Richard never lived with them during the war due to him being called into service.

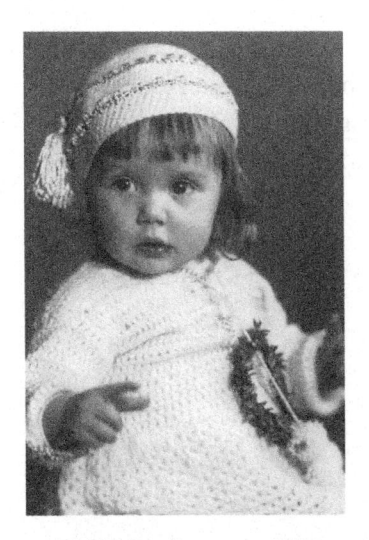

Heidi in her first year, 1936.

Heidi and Tante Hedel at The Mother Eva House, March 1939.

A Child In Berlin

Heidi and Oma at The Mother Eva House, March 1939.

Heidi just after arriving in Berlin, late autumn 1939.

Alfred Machinek, Heidi father, approximately 1939.

Heidi and Käthe, about 1940.

Käthe, Heidi, and Richard, November 1942.

René, around 1947.

René and Heidi, around 1949.

Heidi, New Years Eve, 1953.

Heidi and her St. Bernard Barry in Huntsville, Utah, 1960s.

Heidi in the 1960s.

Heidi on her patio reading letters to the author, Rhonda Lauritzen, 2019.

Heidi in front of the Shooting Star Saloon, which she and her husband John owned, 2023.

CHAPTER EIGHT

1943: TOTAL WAR

THERE HAD BEEN VERY FEW bombings in 1941 and only one in the second half of 1942—mostly just nuisance raids to drop propaganda. So, by the early spring of 1943, Käthe and Heidi had grown used to the calm.

But, although the government would not publicly admit it, losses elsewhere had been devastating. Stalingrad had been a terrible blow. Less than a month before Heidi's seventh birthday, Käthe tuned in to hear Joseph Goebbels give a speech to 14,000 hand-selected, stage-managed faithful Nazis.[1] A commentator before the broadcast described the scene. Draped before the audience, an enormous banner read, "Total War—Shortest War."

Goebbels abandoned his usual optimism; instead, he worked the people into a frenzy.

He roared, "Do you want total war? If necessary, do you want a war more total and radical than anything that we can even imagine today?"

The crowd went wild, shouting, "Yes!"

"Now, people, rise up, and let the storm break loose!"

Millions of Germans tuned in to Goebbels on the radio as he delivered this speech about the "misfortune of the past weeks." He painted an uncharacteristically unvarnished picture of the situation and urged them to sacrifice even more.

---

1   Moorhouse, *Berlin at War*, 339.

Käthe and her friends thought the nation had lost its mind.

Others reacted with sarcasm. The speech led to a joke among people in regions outside Berlin:

> DEAR TOMMY, FLY FURTHER.
>
> WE'RE ALL MINE-WORKERS HERE.
>
> FLY FURTHER TO BERLIN.
>
> THERE, THEY'VE ALL SCREAMED, YES![2]

That speech was a harbinger of the future, the very near future.

On the night of March 1, Berlin shook with the heaviest bombings that had happened yet. Fires burned throughout the city with unusual intensity, including from new bombs known as "blockbusters."

Inside the shelter that night, an old man prattled about the different kinds of bombs. "If you can hear them, you're safe. What should really scare us are the time bombs. The RAF drops them because they want to snuff out the rescue workers. The lucky people will get killed in their sleep. They leave the shelter thinking they are safe, go to bed, and die before they know what hit them. Then, at least, they are free from this nightmare."

The room hushed until someone had the good sense to stop him. "*Halt die schnauze!*" Shut your snout! "There are children here."

When the all-clear sirens blared, people would leave the shelters and walk back tentatively. Did their homes withstand the attack or not? Some people developed rituals, like

---

2   Gamm, Hans-Jochen (1993) [1963]. *Der Flüsterwitz im Dritten Reich [Whispering Jokes in the Third Reich]* (in German). Munich, Zurich: Piper. ISBN 3-492-11417-2.

Frau Schüller across the street, who performed a dance each time her house was still there. Barry was told to sit, and he watched obediently at Herr Schüller's side while the mistress carried on. Heidi never saw Frau and Herr Schüller in the neighborhood shelter. Perhaps they found someone with a well-constructed basement who would let them in with their dog. Heidi stood with Herr Schüller and petted Barry while feeling utter confusion about what was happening to the world, and a pang for pets left behind. When she thought about animals being killed when homes were bombed, she felt angry. Her cat, Ivan, had to be left in the apartment when they went to the shelter. Each time when they returned, they'd find Ivan underneath the sofa quivering with terror. It wasn't right. This was a human war; the animals had nothing to do with it.

Heidi gazed out at the smoke-filled city and then crouched down to confide in Barry. "People say humans are the smart ones but look at this mess and tell me who is dumb. You are a good boy. The best boy."

Sometimes, Heidi really hated the human species.

About 500 citizens were killed that night, and about a hundred thousand people emerged to find their homes destroyed. After being repeatedly told that theirs was the best-defended city in the world, this was a scary new development.

People salvaged what they could before abandoning the rubble. When Heidi and Käthe walked through the city, they saw chalk messages scrawled on the ruins: "All alive in this house. Gone to Frankfurt."

Others wrote platitudes such as, "Our walls might break but not our hearts."

What nonsense, Käthe would say under her breath.

Following the "Total War" speech, a steady convoy of trucks crammed with haggard people rumbled through the neighborhood each day. By then, most of the city's "undesirables" had been "relocated to the east," but now these trucks were full of more privileged Jews, those with Arian spouses, or who had essential jobs such as doctors.

One day, Heidi and Käthe had to pick up some goods on Rosenstrasse, not far from the apartment. When they saw a large group of women gathered outside the Jewish synagogue, Käthe skirted the commotion by going around the block.

Käthe asked Lizzie that night if she knew what was going on.

"Arian women are protesting that their Jewish husbands are being held. I wish to help them but can't risk drawing attention."

That protest was unprecedented and marked a new chapter for Berlin's remaining Jews. Any remaining illusions were shattered if people had been under pretenses that they were safe because of their prominence or Arian spouses.

On March 13, the radio reported that an assassination attempt had been made on Hitler, which would later be known as Operation Valkyrie. Although she didn't say, Käthe was surely disappointed that it was not successful. She wondered what Werner thought about it coming from within the Wehrmacht leadership. She doubted very much that he would have had any involvement if given the opportunity. He would have kept his head down and looked the other way, regardless of his private feelings. Stealing a radio was one thing, attempting a coup was quite another.

Sirens began blaring almost nightly, and Heidi packed a new suitcase to be ready. She chose her best clothes, patent leather shoes, and white socks.

From the time she packed them, she did not wear those items; she just kept them nice inside her suitcase, waiting for better days.

A Child In Berlin

Heidi held her mother's hand while they made their way through the pitch-black city to their neighborhood shelter. Some U-Bahn stations had been damaged by the bigger explosions, Käthe felt safer in the shelters built for the purpose. Inside, large rooms were lined with bunks and stuffed gunny-sack mattresses for the elderly people and children to lie down and sleep.

When a bomb dropped nearby, the ground shook, lights flickered, and the ventilation system brought dust into the rooms. Käthe kept calm during these times, and this was the lead that Heidi followed. She never felt especially frightened. It just became part of life.

Nobody got much rest after spending five hours in shelters many nights of the week, and the whole city of Berlin walked around cranky during the day. It was becoming difficult for Heidi, like other children, to function at school.

Whatever the grownups may have thought of blackout times, darkness was familiar to Heidi. She never related to how other children said they were afraid at night. Instead, it reminded Heidi of the forest and of her Oma. Also, since the war began, she had been trained to feel that the blackout provided cover whereas blaring lights made one vulnerable. The dark felt like a blanket wrapped around her smallness. In it, she could hide from any monster or enemy. Heidi was her mother's *little mouse* who was safe in the crevices, watched over by the moon.

Heidi continued to help her mother's black-market business. One of her jobs was to make paper sacks for dried beans, lentils, or whatever else they had. Her hands learned to work fast, layering, and folding the large sheets into a sturdy funnel shape with flaps folded over the top. They were easy for people to carry and held a lot.

Käthe was always looking over her shoulder in case someone turned them in.

One morning, Heidi spotted a pair of military officers clomping toward the building. Heidi had been trained to alert her mother, so she hurried home, and they scrambled to hide evidence.

But the men were not police or Gestapo; they were military and were coming to collect Frau Schüller's son from across the street. His doctor had deemed him fit for duty again, and they were there to bring him to the front. What a cruel trick to let someone come home and rest, only to remove him again.

Frau Schüller and her husband closed the door, and they were not seen outside much after that. Barry still went out for the day's rolls and Heidi waited for him to come out to say hello, but after his job was done, they let him back in straightaway and he seldom went back out.

Within a few weeks, Frau Schüller told Käthe she had received *the letter*.

The strange thing was that she had already sensed the letter was on its way. How had she known?

One night as she slept, she heard her name spoken aloud clearly. She jolted upright from a dead sleep. Somehow, she knew that her son had taken his last breath.

The letter followed and stopped her from wondering. She had been right.

When Heidi learned the news, she thought of him reading stories to her, and she wept for another person who had died. She wept for her neighbors.

How many people must she lose? She imagined the young soldier becoming an angel like the hunchback from the story.

■ ■ ■

By May, the Nazi Navy suffered devastating losses in the Atlantic. Their "wolf pack" U-boats were defeated, and

Admiral Karl Dönitz called off operations there rather than suffer further disaster. It became known as "Black May."

Käthe was more aware than the average person because although propaganda sources stopped talking about it, she heard censored news on the shortwave radio. She understood that the war was not going in Germany's favor after Stalingrad or in the Atlantic.

She began letting herself hope that it would be over soon.

Then, as they ate breakfast one morning, they heard a loud rapping on the door, shouting, *"Gestapo! Aufmachen!"* (Gestapo! Open up!)

When Heidi came out, her mother had already answered the door calmly. A man was wearing a long leather coat, with two others flanking him behind. Her mother smiled and responded compliantly, diffusing tension with her natural charm.

The man walked through the apartment, and Heidi thought he must enjoy the way his footsteps made a commanding sound on the floor, letting the whole building know he was there. He opened closets and cupboards, and Heidi went pale thinking about a suitcase full of black-market fabric along with their pretty white curtains. The suitcase lay on the floor, and while the man's back was turned, Heidi gently slid it under the couch with her foot. He returned from the bedroom with bolts of cloth from the wardrobe, which he placed into a box and glued an eagle and swastika seal to prevent it from being opened.

Then, he said someone would return to confiscate it the following day, and the men left without finding the case under the couch.

After he left, Käthe steamed the seal off and removed about a third of the fabric. Her mouth had a sly half-smile while she worked. Then she pasted the seal back on with no trace of tampering.

That evening, Käthe arranged for Heidi to stay with a neighbor "In case they take me to Alex." She was referring to the police headquarters called Polizeipräsidium, which people usually referred to as "Alex," or sometimes "The fortress on Alex," because it was located at Alexanderplatz. The imposing and unattractive red brick building was visible from their apartment window.

The following day, the Gestapo did come again to retrieve the fabric, and they gave Käthe a few minutes to place Heidi with Frau Pohl upstairs. Käthe assured the girl, "I won't be gone long. A day or two."

She was calm and smiling for Heidi's benefit. This made Heidi believe her. And Käthe had reason to believe it herself. Having a few bolts of black-market fabric was a petty offense, and she knew others who had been interrogated for similar infractions that included things like failing to Heil Hitler, not singing patriotic songs at the right time, or possessing contraband.

Heidi spent hours staring out the window at "Alex," wondering if her mother was okay inside there.

True to her word, Käthe returned two days later. She looked frazzled but otherwise seemed the same as before, brushing off any questions and acting like nothing had happened. Only two things changed. The first was that Käthe set aside a big piece of red fabric for her own use. She stood in front of the mirror, draping it around her body and imagining it as a dress. Nobody wore anything extravagant those days, and so Käthe dreamed of celebrating when the war was over. Dreams were a form of defiance.

The other change was that Käthe began role-playing with Heidi about how to answer questions that someone might ask.

There was only one correct answer, "I don't know."

They practiced conversations at random times, with her mother deliberately trying to catch Heidi off guard.

"What is your name?"

"Heidi."

"No! You say, 'I don't know.' Where do you live? Who is your mother? You answer, 'I don't know.'"

Heidi protested, "But people will think I am dumb."

Her mother responded, "The only dumb thing is answering questions. I don't care what anyone thinks, and neither should you. Life is at stake."

They continued the game until Heidi's responses became automatic.

In late July, a stream of refugees with bedraggled clothes and vacant looks came through Anhalter station from Hamburg as they were being sent east for rehousing. Those who stopped told anyone who would listen what had happened there. Their stories were so horrifying they seemed hard to believe. Incendiary bombs had created a sea of flames that consumed the city. People were stuck in melting asphalt or asphyxiated in bunkers below.

An evacuation order came on August 1, 1943, for all women and children to leave Berlin. Käthe had vowed she would not send Heidi away again, but her stay at the police station and the recent news from Hamburg had rattled her. Her shortwave radio had prepared her to accept that war could surely come to the ground in Berlin, and it would be much safer for Heidi to not be there. And if Käthe were called in again by the Gestapo, she might not get a slap on the wrist. Käthe shuddered to think what might happen if she were in jail and had to leave Heidi alone.

When Käthe told Heidi her plan to send Heidi to stay in the Czech countryside with Tante Hedel and her husband, Heidi begged, "Mútti, come with me."

But Käthe only responded, "I can't. People need me here."

That was a bitter thought. *Who needs you more than me?* Heidi was stoic about what had to be done; everyone was stoic in those days. But it still hurt every time her mother left her.

Käthe would at least accompany Heidi to Sudetenland and would not leave until she was satisfied it was a good situation with Tante Hedel. She would not make that mistake again. At least Heidi would be with family, and Oma was not so far away if needed.

Uschi did not take the news well. "You are lucky you are getting out of this trash heap of a city. Take me with you."

Heidi hugged her, "I wish I could. I'll be back before you know it. I always end up back here."

Now Uschi was crying, "I don't believe you. People go away and that's the last you hear. War takes everything good."

Heidi hugged her and said, "Watch some movies for me. I won't be seeing any for a while."

"We will be here until the last bomb falls," Uschi said.

Before Heidi and her mother left for the train, Heidi picked up Ivan and rubbed her nose to his. "Be a good cat, and don't cause trouble with the neighbors." Uschi had agreed to take care of him until Käthe returned.

When they arrived, Hedel looked well. She had a one-year-old daughter named Ereka now, and Heidi would be a good help. It was nearly the harvest season. There were many animals in the surrounding farms that Heidi could go see: chickens, rabbits, and pigs—although the piglets they kept had grown beyond the play stage by that time of year.

Heidi adjusted to her new surroundings. This time, she had a history of coping. It was easier in every way except for reopening the wound of being left behind. After her arrival, she started having the recurring nightmare of her mother and the coffin again. Heidi also felt deeply embarrassed that she was still wetting the bed, and so she slept on straw that could be rinsed and dried in the sun. She regularly hand-rinsed her own bedsheets.

Once she fell into a routine, however, Heidi realized it was a relief to rest from the air raids. She was used to Berlin, but now this calm contrast pointed out how scary the air raids had been. In the quiet countryside, Heidi caught up on sleep in no time. She also loved being back in a village, seeing the night sky, and having animals as playmates. Yes, she missed her friends, but she could be patient to spend time with other children once school started in the fall.

And although no country under the Reich's authority had it easy, Czechs were allies and they were treated far better than Poles.

A week after arriving, Tante Hedel brought Heidi into a meadow where she spread freshly boiled bedsheets flat to bleach in the sun. She taught Heidi how to sprinkle them from a watering can, which promoted the bleaching process. Heidi's job was to stay the whole day and keep birds or animals from landing on the clean linens. While tending the linens, she made garlands of flowers to wear as she passed the time. This was a routine that Tante Hedel had done herself about once a month, and now she was grateful to have Heidi's help with the chore.

That night, Tante Hedel rewarded Heidi by taking her into the forest.

They walked past other farmers' lands, and Heidi asked, "Why do they put *der mist*, the dung pile, out in front for everyone to smell? Why don't they hide it?"

Hedel laughed. "Men need to show off whose is bigger. The higher the heap, the wealthier they are."

In the forest, they gathered wild mushrooms, and Heidi absorbed the smell of freshly cut wood. She thought of her father, the Czech woodsman who grew up not far from there.

As night fell, they put up two hammocks: one for Tante Hedel and the baby and the other for Heidi. After a while, however, their hammocks began to slump. And then, they heard something grunting and pawing at the ground. Wild boars had sniffed them out, perhaps hoping they might scavenge for scraps. They were far too close for comfort, so they decided to abandon that plan. Instead, they climbed a nearby forest ranger's tower where they could spread their beds on the platform. High above the pine trees and ancient oaks, Heidi fell asleep happy.

She and Tante Hedel loved that night so much that they began making a habit of it once a week or so until the weather chilled. Whenever they saw the forest ranger, they talked with him, and he seemed pleased to have willing pupils, telling them all about the trees and animals. Those carefree nights were among the happiest of Heidi's whole childhood.

That fall, Heidi started second grade. She trudged a few kilometers along dirt roads, gathering up with other children along the way. Horse-drawn hay wagons sometimes passed them, kicking up a cloud of dust into which the children would disappear and hitch a ride on the back. If the farmer heard them giggling or spotted one hanging off the side, he'd flick his long whip backward to make them jump off. After a rain, the roads turned into thick mud, so the children tromped across weeds along the side.

Heidi was happy to be back in school with other children, but it was difficult since she did not speak the Czech language very well. Teachers equated that with a lack of intelligence, labeling her not very bright.

Rather than stoop to their expectations, Heidi's instinct was to rebel. She told herself, "I will show myself what I can do." She listened hard and was soon speaking fluently, although reading was more difficult.

After supper in the evenings, they'd click on the radio for news of the war. The Americans, whom they called *Amis*, and Russians, whom they called *Ruskies*, were gathering momentum. Most people in Tante Hedel's circles no longer believed the Germans would win, so it was a race to see whether the Amis or Ruskies would make it to Berlin first. The Ruskies were widely feared, and people hoped it would be the Amis.

They also heard on the radio about the terrible time that Berlin was experiencing. That November, heavy bombings rained fire, and Heidi's stomach knotted with worry for her mother. That month, about half a million Berliners were rendered homeless, about 10,000 were injured, and 3,500 were killed. In addition, many important buildings were bombed, including the Staatsoper, which had already been rebuilt once, and the zoo was destroyed. Nearly all the remaining animals were killed in a single night. Their carcasses were gathered and butchered to provide meat to a citizenry who had tasted precious little protein in previous months.

A month later, Tante Hedel took Heidi to Oma's for Christmas, and Käthe met them there. Oma shook her head in astonishment at the passage of time as measured in Heidi's growth. She was tall for her age and her once-plump elbows and knees had elongated into bony limbs. She still had round cheeks and a dimpled smile, though.

Käthe brought an update about Uschi, "She is doing fine, but she asks about you at least once a day," Käthe laughed.

She also brought the best gift Heidi could have wished for—her cat Ivan. Presents were hard to come by anyway, and Heidi would not have imagined anything better. Käthe may not have been only thinking of Heidi's morale. The hungrier people got in the city, the fewer pets were seen in Berlin.

When it was time to leave, Oma again extended the plea to let Heidi stay there, especially since Tante Lucy was now married and settled elsewhere. This time, Käthe did not give a blanket "no." Instead, she told Oma that she would *think about it*.

Käthe did express the reasons she thought it was best for Heidi to remain with Hedel. Heidi had just settled into school and was getting the language well now. Uprooting her yet again would be unnecessarily stressful. There was also the fact that Heidi had proven to be a real help for Hedel and the baby.

Soon after the cat arrived, however, he discovered that the neighbor's baby chicks make delightful prey. She heard her uncle swearing at the animal, and Heidi begged her pet to be a good boy. But Ivan was not an obedient kitty.

Then one day, Heidi could not find him anywhere. So, she asked her family if they had seen Ivan.

Her uncle said, "He's in there," and pointed to the dinner pot where a stew was cooking. They were not really having cat for dinner, but he had lassoed Ivan earlier that day after their angry neighbor reported more dead chicks. Ivan had choked to death.

A wave of nausea passed over her, followed by grief. Another friend dead. Heidi's heartbreak did not pass quickly. Neither did her resentment.

Not long after that, Heidi developed a boil on her head that grew so large it was painful to the touch. Hedel did not know what to do with her, so she sent Heidi to Oma's house. Heidi was overjoyed, and so was Oma. They had both been waiting for that day to come for years, and Heidi nuzzled into the soft warmth of Oma's middle-aged stoutness. Heidi felt that she was home at last, and she intended to stay there. Maybe forever.

CHAPTER NINE

1944:
RETURNING TO THE VILLAGE, THEN BACK TO BERLIN

A FIRST ORDER OF BUSINESS was for Oma to try drawing out the infection with a poultice. When that didn't work, Heidi had to visit a doctor. She resisted, remembering the little boy with the round face. But Oma promised she would not leave her side. It was the only doctor visit Heidi would have in her entire childhood.

The doctor lanced it and drained the fluid. It was a messy affair, but it eased the pressure, and her wound healed quickly after that, now aided by Oma's poultice that kept the infection out.

Although Heidi had grown to enjoy Berlin, she now cherished this time back with her grandparents. She took up her old bed in the kitchen, which had a big box underneath for Opa's cobbler supplies. He'd pulled up a milk stool in front of an anvil that he swapped out with various sizes of shoes. To re-sole boots, he traced an outline, then removed the worn-out sole and glued a new one to it. Next, he shaped leather, punched holes in it, and fastened slipper uppers to a sole with wooden dowels not much thicker than a toothpick.

Each Saturday, Heidi helped Oma to clean the house from top to bottom, which included scrubbing the wood floors with sand and a stiff brush and cleaning the silverware with a paste made from wood ash.

They always had enough to eat. Sometimes, Oma made shredded potato pancakes. She added an egg to bind it, then a little salt and pepper, or she served it sprinkled with sugar for dessert. But Heidi's favorite meal during that time was Oma's sour rye soup that took several days to ferment, served with crusty bread.

Oma also took the opportunity to tutor Heidi on her knitting, teaching her how to work fast, never taking the yarn out of her hand, knitting on one side, and purling on the other. It would take many years before Heidi could match Oma's speed, though. Oma could knit Heidi a new pair of mittens in the time it took Heidi to take a nap.

When they went into town, they sometimes bought a Polish kielbasa to eat on the way home. "Don't tell Opa," she would say.

Heidi often arose early and went to mass with Oma, just to be near her. Praying for her mother and for the war to end also seemed like a good idea. She never missed mass on Sundays. She noticed how different things were in the city compared to the village. Her mother and the men she had dated were affectionate and talkative, like best friends. Men and women mingled in groups, so different from the way the men and women sat in separate sections at church in the village. Oma and Opa had a practical relationship and were not the kind of people who held hands or showed affection to each other. They talked about household matters, but Heidi never saw them laughing or having earnest conversations. Their relationship did not seem tense; it was simply that men and women had different lives.

But although Heidi could not bring herself to admit it, she was growing bored with her grandparents. Her older uncle Edward picked on her, but he was a teenager now and so most of the time, he was working in his job as a butcher's apprentice. As a result, Heidi craved friends and other activities.

And so, when early summer came, Oma planned a little trip. The two walked an entire day to get to her sister's house. Oma's sister was twenty years younger and so she had several children only a little older than Heidi. Oma and Heidi had only planned to stay over for two days before returning home, but Heidi was having such a marvelous time with her cousins that Oma could see a longing look on the girl's face. She asked if Heidi would like to stay. Heidi did not want to hurt Oma's feelings, but Oma could see the answer.

"You can remain here for a while, and I will check on you often."

The cottage had been larger at one time, but a few years ago, lightning struck and killed Oma's brother-in-law. No one else was injured, but it burned the main part of the house. Oma's sister and the children made do by constructing a new cottage using part of a barn that had a horse and cow stall in it. In this way, they could share the use of one wall, relying on the support of an existing structure. They salvaged everything possible from the old home, creating an odd mishmash of walls and materials.

There was a bedroom and a *gute stube*, or "good room," where the children were not allowed. The kitchen shared the wall with the horse stall. That wall had an original window that used to let light into the barn. So now, Heidi's seat at the table faced the window, and she'd eat supper while staring at the horse and cow. She thought it was marvelous. Except for all the flies.

There was no running water inside. Instead, culinary water came from a deep well carried inside with a pail.

Heidi adored being around the other children, and they all slept in the barn on beds made of fresh hay. They seemed to enjoy that arrangement, and Heidi did, too.

A litter of kittens was just getting to the cute stage, so Heidi and the others were allowed to choose a kitten to sleep with at night.

Heidi was assigned to scrub the piglet stalls clean, then add fresh straw. Once that job was done, the piglets went in, and the children jumped into the straw after them. Then, when the piglets were weaned, she could choose one of them to sleep with her. Heidi felt she was in heaven.

Oma visited to check on Heidi but found her healthy and happy there. She decided to let her stay for the rest of the summer.

By the harvest season of 1944, the fields were cut, and the children ran through the stubble one day. Heidi was barefoot as usual. However, when she climbed onto a large rock with the rest of her cousins, they noticed blood dripping from her feet. She was having such a good time that she hardly minded, but her adult cousin Agnes felt bad about it, and tore up an apron to bandage Heidi's feet for the walk home.

While the fall weather was still warm, Käthe came to get her. Käthe had resigned herself earlier that year to leaving Heidi in the safety of the countryside for as long as possible. But now Käthe believed it was only a matter of time before the German stronghold crumbled. The situation was changing rapidly, and she had to calculate the risks.

Käthe understood that the cost of staying in the village could end up being too high a price. The Russians were advancing farther west each day, and they would surely overrun the village. She did not want either of them to be there when that happened. She mistrusted the Germans, but she was terrified of Russian revenge.

Käthe believed the Americans would surely get to Berlin before the Russians did, and she decided to bet on that. If the Americans took over, then Berlin would be the best place for them. Not only that, but cities usually evacuated their women and children before ground fighting closed in. So Käthe would listen to the shortwave radio, and they would head west into an American zone if the Russians got anywhere close.

And so it was settled. Käthe and Heidi would return together. She resolved that it was the last time she would let her daughter out of her care.

Before returning to Berlin, Heidi and her mother got to sleep in the good room that night, which made Heidi feel special. As they snuggled into bed, back in each other's arms, Käthe discovered the next plague that had descended on her daughter: fleas.

Käthe shook her head and said, "My little mouse, by the time you are married you will have forgotten all these troubles."

■ ■ ■

When the train pulled into Anhalter station, Heidi was shocked at the contrast between her first vivid memories. They debarked into the open air because the vast awning was now reduced to a few spans of rusting metal and shards where glass panes had been. The once-elegant frontage was now sandbagged, and people ignored the propaganda posters.

Instead, some subversives had begun scrawling Hitler's 1933 campaign slogan on bombed-out buildings. "Give me four more years, and you will not recognize Germany."

They arrived at the Alexanderplatz station a few minutes later, and Heidi felt happy to be back in her old stomping grounds. But as they picked their way home, Heidi's mouth gaped open when she reflexively looked up to see the giant Berolina statue, but instead, her eyes found daylight.

When Käthe noticed Heidi's finger pointing at what wasn't there, she shrugged. "They said she is gone for safekeeping."

But Heidi heard doubt in her mother's voice. The statue was not safe.

Heidi gawked at Berolina's empty stage; it felt like the city's protector was gone.

Once inside the apartment, Heidi reflexively expected to be greeted by her cat but then felt a bitter pang at remembering his death. Grief washed over her by surprise.

She sighed, "I miss Ivan."

That night, Lizzie came over, unable to wait before sharing her news with Käthe.

"*He's alive*," she whispered, breathless. "At a work detail associated with Sachsenhausen."[1]

Käthe and Lizzie held each other and wept with the hope that Lizzie's boyfriend might be assigned to duty where his mind was an asset.

"If he can just last a little longer, then the war will be over," Lizzie said.

The next day Heidi could not wait to check on Uschi. Heidi bounded upstairs and was greeted by Uschi's mother. The woman had always been shy, but now she looked drawn and shell-shocked. Despite that, her face lit up to see Heidi, and she threw her arms around the girl.

"I am happy to see you looking healthy. Your family has kept you fed."

Heidi had never known Uschi's mom to be affectionate like that, but the return of anyone in those days was a precious gift. Uschi came running with open arms and red hair looking like it was aflame.

---

1 The camp where he was sent is speculative based on Heidi overhearing the grownups discuss Sachsenhausen during this time and our triangulation of other facts.

Uschi looked taller, which made her seem stretched out and lanky. She was ten now, and her mother had shrunk next to her. Looking at the color in Uschi's cheeks and how sallow her mother was, Heidi could tell who was eating the rations and who was going without.

"I have loads to show you."

No school was happening that fall, as social institutions were crumbling. Also, most of the city's children had already been evacuated. So, Uschi and a group of preteen boys who remained had unfettered time each day to play and scavenge for treasures.

"I'll get you in with them," she assured Heidi. "They do whatever I say."

Heidi doubted that, but she let Uschi have her fantasy.

Uschi led Heidi on a guided tour of the newest sights in a cityscape that looked like a different place.

First, Uschi showed Heidi her shrapnel collection from the flak guns. These twisted bits of metal were a hot commodity for trading with other children who collected the most unusual pieces.

Next, she led Heidi to Alexanderplatz, where Berolina had been, but Heidi said, "I saw already."

Uschi leaned in as if to tell a secret, "I hear they melted her for bullets to shoot the Russians."

This hurt Heidi's heart. She had loved that statue in a similar way that she loved Oma's heirloom Christmas ornaments. She felt like they were part of what made their family special. Each year when the ornaments came out of the box, Heidi was as excited to see them as an old friend. Heidi had never realized how an empty space could feel so tangible. It was like the absence was a thing itself, and this was how she had felt when she entered the apartment and Ivan was not there. It just seemed wrong to melt the statue down, like how it was wrong to kill a pet.

Next, Uschi headed to surprise Heidi with their gang's newest find, but just before they rounded the corner, Uschi warned her. "Don't look at the ground on your right."

As she said it, a putrid smell wafted toward them.

Heidi instinctively looked and saw a dead airman lying in a pool of his own blood. The blood was dried and black. He was bloated and purple, and flies covered his flesh.

Heidi had to quell her gag reflex, and Uschi clucked, "I told you not to look."

Heidi turned away and then spotted an airplane wing that had fallen from the sky. This was the surprise.

The wide end was wedged between debris, making it able to flex. Uschi climbed up and demonstrated what she and the others had discovered to do with it. Uschi jumped hard, which made the wing flex and spring back up.

"Hop on!" she called to Heidi.

Heidi did, and the two jumped in unison to get the wing to bend lower, then fling them higher.

They did that for a while until a pack of older boys showed up.

One called to Uschi, "Who said you could bring a friend?"

"Heidi will help us," Uschi vouched.

"Let's see about that," the leader said. "We found something else."

The leader (who was, in fact, *not* Uschi) showed them to a newly bombed-out building that had been a grocery.

One boy scouted the perimeter and then hollered, "Look, there's an opening here!"

It was a small hole covered up by a heap of rubble, but it was clearly a blown-out window. This was promising. So, they quickly assembled a line to pass chunks of concrete out of the way, bucket brigade style. They had seen that procedure plenty of times by adults. An hour later, they had opened a hole big enough for the smallest of them to fit through.

"You're up, Schnuckiputzi," one of the boys elbowed Heidi in the ribs.

Heidi took her orders and within minutes had wormed her way through feet-first while hanging onto the windowsill. She lowered herself down and then let herself drop into the dark basement. Her heart pounded, and she hoped the building would not come down on her head.

It took a while for Heidi's eyes to adjust to the dimness, but eventually, she glanced around. It was a single room with shelves, apparently for holding inventory. The shelves were mostly bare, but she picked her way around debris until she found what must have been the owner's most prized stash back in a corner: two salamis and three large tins of butter cookies.

"I can't believe my eyes!" Heidi yelled out.

"Tell us!"

Heidi joked, "I'm going to make you wait while I enjoy a reward for risking my life."

They groaned and yelled threats if she didn't share.

"I'm kidding. You will see."

She carried the first salami and dragged a chair to the wall, then pushed the salami outside. They roared with delight, passing it around so everyone could sniff it before eating any.

"There are two more," she told them. "Swear to me you will save my share, or I will eat the best down here by myself."

After becoming convinced of their promises, Heidi pushed out the other salami and the cookie tins. Then, standing on the chair, she gave them her hands, and they pulled her out as her toes searched for a grip on the foundation. By the time Heidi was on the street, she was covered in dust, and her limbs were scraped up from going through the hole. But she had earned her place in the group, and they would all eat well today.

They spirited their loot away to an abandoned building away from prying eyes. They ate half of a salami and one tin of cookies on the spot, then divided the rest for their families.

They were well-practiced, and there was no squabbling other than some banter about how the kid who made the salami cuts was favoring himself.

It had been a good day, and she felt proud of herself.

Heidi did her best to clean up before going home, but Käthe took one look and folded her arms. "This is how you come back on your first day home?"

But before Käthe could complain further, Heidi presented the salami and cookies.

Käthe's eyes sparkled at the sight. "Where did you get these?"

"From a bombed-out shop."

Käthe did not know whether to dance with delight or to lecture.

She bit her lip and left it at, "Promise me to be careful."

"*Of course!*" Heidi thought she had been.

From then on, Heidi, Uschi, and the others spent their days scavenging for food and mischief. Housewives still sent them to fetch the day's rations, and Heidi was now skilled at dickering on how much she would be paid, first shrugging her shoulders like she was more interested in playing than standing in line all day. When the price was worth her while, she accepted the job and trotted off with Uschi so they could keep each other entertained while waiting in the queue. Heidi and her friends had unparalleled freedom, and they enjoyed the feeling of control over their domain. That control was in stark contrast to how little of it they had over so much else. What else could they do but amuse themselves?

One sad development during the time Heidi had been away was that Frau and Herr Schüller boarded up their home and left with Barry. What a lonesome thought it was that she never got to say goodbye.

When Heidi asked about them, Käthe answered, "Frau Schüller's nerves were shot."

One day, the boys in Heidi and Uschi's gang bounded off to a fresh bomb crater, eager to show Heidi and Uschi their latest find. Others were already in the pit clawing out treasures that were buried deep in the archaeology layers. Heidi saw a boy holding a human skull that looked to have been in the ground for at least a century. They heaped it onto a big pile whenever they pulled out a bone.

This crater was in the courtyard of a home for old people, and the kids figured there must have once been a cemetery.

Heidi and Uschi sorted bones into piles, "I've got a finger."

"This is a thigh bone."

The boys mostly ignored the other bones because they were hunting for skulls.

Then, one boy halted the excavations and gathered everyone around for the show. He poured gunpowder into the eye sockets, then made a fuse from string and lit it. They cheered when the skull exploded. The boys were constantly prowling for items to blow up since gunpowder was one commodity *not* in short supply. All they had to do was collect it for free from spent machine gun bullets that littered the ground around the flak towers. Many still contained a little gunpowder, which they poured into containers. Occasionally, they also pilfered live ammunition off dead airmen.

Heidi thought this activity was great fun, not giving a second thought to the right-or-wrongness of blowing up skulls. It was a treasure hunt that felt like they were on an Egyptian dig or had found a pirate's lair. Diversions like this were especially welcome because they kept hunger pangs out of mind for a while.

Food was becoming terribly scarce and people did everything they could to get more. Rabbits were known as "balcony pigs" as a protein source, and residents swept dust into pots to grow vegetables. They made garden plots in the open spaces of courtyards or bay windows. People with city gardens had always gathered horse droppings from the beer wagon Clydesdales, but those animals were gone now, too. They could not be fed and so had been put down and butchered. Then, bedraggled people stood in lines for meat rations, appreciative of something they wouldn't have dreamed of eating before the war.

One evening, Käthe cooked up a rabbit for dinner, but a few days later, she confided in Heidi, "I'm not sure that was a rabbit."

Heidi shook her head as if to tell her mother she didn't want to know, but Käthe couldn't help herself, like if she said it aloud it wouldn't be true. "The head and the feet had been removed. I fear it was a cat."

It was too late to worry, and maybe it was best they hadn't known it at the time. They needed what they could get.

Käthe now dealt mainly in bags of beans, dried lentils, or peas, and she started acquiring beautiful things in exchange for these as people in the city traded possessions for food.

Sometimes while walking through the streets, the whiff of a decaying or charred body was foul enough to knock a person over. It wasn't only garden plots that were in high demand, but it was getting harder to bury the dead. People always found a way to lay their own families to rest, even if they had to bury them in a park. But British airmen were often left to rot, and it was not always possible to pull bodies from the rubble. There was so much death that it became a pervasive stench. Nobody got used to it.

A Child In Berlin

One night after an air raid, Käthe and Heidi returned to their bed. Several hours later, the neighborhood shook and trembled. The next day, Heidi learned that a time bomb had gone off, blowing up the home of one of the boys in her group. Everyone in that apartment building had been killed in their sleep.

This family had simply been alive one moment and dead the next. Heidi hoped it had been quick, but she couldn't stop her mind from wondering how long it takes to die. If you are killed instantly, do you know what is happening when the angels come to get you? Or do you have time to think about dying before it is all over? How much do you suffer? She hoped it was over in an instant. That would be a lot better than the awful moaning she heard from Uschi's father as he lay dying for all those months. Yes, better to get it done with, especially if you go out with your whole family at once. Surviving alone might be the worst of all.

■ ■ ■

Käthe and Heidi continued to listen to their shortwave radio, which told them where air raids were coming from. If they learned it was the Russians, they no longer bothered going to the shelters. It was the British and American planes that really damaged the city. Käthe could also tell the source of the bombers based on how they sounded. She joked that the Russian planes rattled and shook so much they must be made of plywood.

By now, it was early December, and Käthe got word from Richard that he had a few days of leave after he had finished his training and was on his way to his assignment. So Käthe dressed herself up and got Heidi ready to bid him farewell.

He entered the apartment carrying a package for Käthe, "This is an early Christmas present. Open it now."

She did, and Heidi's eyes widened when she saw the contents: a generous package of snow-white sugar, some fluffy white flour, a tin of lard, and three eggs.

He said, "Don't sell or trade this. I want you to enjoy it when I am gone."

Käthe looked radiant, flush with happiness, not just because of the sugar and flour. She gazed at Richard fondly.

Käthe said, "We will bake a cake on Christmas."

They still had some brown beet sugar for trading, but to possess nearly all the ingredients they needed for a real cake and in time for Christmas was a true gift. In that dreary time, it was not only the thing itself but the gift of having something to look forward to. It was a reminder that there are good things in the world and that Christmas was still a time of celebration and light.

Heidi stayed with Frau Pohl for the next two nights, giving the adults some alone time before Richard had to ship out.

After he left, they ate one of the three eggs for supper and preserved the other two in a box of wall plaster powder for later.

On December 6, Käthe directed Heidi to shine her shoes and set them out. Heidi could only imagine what St. Nicolas might be able to find in those times, but she went to sleep excited.

The following day, she was delighted to get a magazine. It was out of date and had probably been passed through several hands before reaching Heidi, but she didn't care. She could make paper dolls with it. There were no treats to eat, but Heidi had not expected any. She cherished it.

The magazine made her remember that she had not seen her *Max and Moritz* book in quite a while and so she asked her mother.

"Where were you when you last read it?"

Heidi could not quite remember.

Later that day, Heidi and her mother made an outing to see their cousin Agnes, who had just arrived in the city. They traveled about ten kilometers northeast, to a neighborhood known as Hohenschönhausen. Upon arrival, Agnes hugged them both and remarked on how Heidi had changed just since the previous summer.

"How are your feet?" She asked, recalling the day when Heidi had bloodied her feet scampering through the cut fields.

Käthe brought some dried beans wrapped in paper as a gift, and the two settled in to talk.

Agnes said, "I thought you had the right idea to come west before the war ends."

Käthe asked, "What do you hear about the Jews?"

Agnes sighed, "They are all gone from the villages now. There are big compounds where Jews come in by the trainload. The only thing that seems to leave those places is acrid smoke."

Käthe shuddered. "I know people in those camps."

Agnes nodded. She did, too.

Käthe prodded her cousin for information, "Do you think the Ruskies, or the Amis will make it here first?"

Agnes said, "The Amis. But I am hedging my bets." She fingered a red tablecloth she had set out for the holiday.

She went on, "In my trunk, my Christmas ornaments were wrapped in this. Nobody would think a Christmas cloth is political. If the Russians get here first, I will hang it outside or wear it if we need to flee."

Käthe nodded her approval. It was a smart strategy, better than a white flag.

Agnes continued, whispering, "This neighborhood is stuffed with communists. If the Russians beat the Amis, word has it, they will come through this neighborhood first."

People here will let them right in. I do not think there will be much fighting. This will be the safest place in Berlin."

Käthe nodded. "Heidi and I will be long gone by then. We have a shortwave radio, and if the Ruskies get within two weeks' march of this city, we will leave for Stuttgart. I have a friend there." The friend she was referring to was Lizzie. Her apartment had been bombed a while earlier, and so she left for Stuttgart a while earlier with Wolfgang in tow.

During the holidays, Käthe had a male friend come over, Jarda. He was one of the more fortunate foreign workers, a Czech who had come voluntarily early in the war because he had a special skill: making dentures and bridges. This profession was in very high demand,[2] and it afforded him a comfortable civilian life in the city.

He was tall, broad-shouldered, and had thick, dark blonde hair with deep blue eyes. Heidi thought he was the best-looking of her previous boyfriends—even better than Werner, and she had liked Werner.

While he worked at a dentist's office, he often brought wax molds to the apartment so he could get extra work done there without being seen. This was where he could do black-market jobs in trade for valuable goods, or to help people who were excluded from official dentists. His false teeth were worth a lot on the black market, and so he could work as many hours as there were in a day. In the apartment, he disconnected the gas cooktop and used the flame to melt and shape the wax.

---

2   During World War II, it was common for adults of any age to wear dentures, which often got lost, broken, or were ill-fitting. Mobile dental units were a necessary part of all military groups. Dentistry and the making of false teeth were also an important profession in civilian life, and many dentists and technicians would have been away serving as part of the war effort. Thus, Jarda was a prime example of the great many foreign workers brought in to fill in Germany's labor shortage on the home front. Heidi remembers watching him work.

A Child In Berlin

One night, during an air raid, people could not get into the shelter fast enough as the sky lit up with triangular-shaped flares people called "Christmas Trees." These dropped from planes so bombardiers could see their targets, and they were illuminating all four corners of a nearby block. People began pushing, and someone was trampled to death. It was not the first time, and it spooked Käthe.

It was one of the few times Heidi ever saw panic on her mother's face, and it frightened her. The next day, Käthe told Jarda what happened. After that, they only went to the big, purpose-built bunkers if they were worried about a bombardment being an especially bad one. If they suspected that a severe attack might be coming, Jarda would stay on the sofa so they could go to a big shelter together and he could help protect them. He would put Heidi on his shoulders safely out of the trample zone. Although Heidi was eight, she didn't weigh much. One time, the press of people got so bad Jarda had to walk backward, keeping his face to the crowd, holding his umbrella out in front to keep them at bay.

■ ■ ■

On Christmas Eve, there were no trees to be found, and Käthe and Heidi had no gifts to give each other. But they had enough for a cake, and they had been looking forward to this ever since Richard had left them with the ingredients. Heidi helped her mother mix the batter, and then their cake went into the oven. They were happy working together as a team.

The smell of the baking cake drove them wild. At last, they removed it from the oven and did not wait until it cooled. Käthe drizzled a syrup-like mixture on top, which soaked in and moistened the cake. Then Käthe placed two large slices on plates.

"*Frohe Weihnachten.*" Merry Christmas. Käthe slid a piece to Heidi.

Their mouths watered as they raised the first bite. Then Heidi's face scrunched, and she spat the cake out. She looked up to see her mother do the same. It was awful, like eating pure salt.

What had gone wrong?

Käthe went to the kitchen, trailed her finger inside the measuring cup, and tasted it. Salt.

They figured out that Heidi had seen the jar of salt, thought it was sugar, and added salt…in the sugar quantity. Käthe had already added the sugar.

They spent all their ingredients on this single Christmas extravagance and couldn't eat any of it.

Heidi's face flushed with shame, and involuntary tears flooded her eyes. "I am so sorry, Mútti. So sorry. I have ruined our Christmas."

Käthe was stricken, and she couldn't look at the cake or her daughter. She stiffened, picked up the plate, then slid their precious cake into the rubbish bin. Then, grabbing a kitchen rag, she cleaned up their baking mess. She couldn't speak.

"Mútti, let me help."

"You've done enough. We cannot afford mistakes."

Heidi slumped to bed, face down and wrenched with guilt.

As Käthe scrubbed, she muttered. "We must hold ourselves upright. No mistakes. No mistakes."

But the more she willed her strength to harden, the more brittle it became. A minute later, her resolve cracked and she crumbled into a pile of grief.

Heidi could hear her mother sobbing in great torrents of emotion.

That night, they could not comfort one another, their pain too solitary and too acute. There was nothing to be done, no bright side, and no seeming end to the hell that Berlin had become.

On Christmas Day, Käthe stayed in bed until noon, and Heidi tidied the apartment while giving her mother a wide berth. The two did not speak a word that day.

The day after that, Käthe arose fresh, dressed, and kissed Heidi on her head. "Be good, little mouse. I will see you at dinner. Jarda is coming over."

They never spoke of the cake.

That night, Jarda came over and brought some liquor.

"We must toast to today. That is all we know."

They drank on empty stomachs and soon were laughing.

Heidi caught the way her mother looked at Jarda. There was a glint of longing in her eyes that she hadn't seen since Werner. Maybe she had never seen her mother wear that look.

Her mother clicked on the radio to music, and Jarda took her hand to dance. Heidi observed them, and the memory of melting ice cream cones from the movie came to her mind.

On New Year's Eve, Käthe hosted a small celebration with her best friends, which was not quite as lively without Lizzie.

When Jarda entered the apartment, he looked hungrily at Käthe. "You look ravishing."

Käthe joked. "I took a shower just for you."

The others glanced at her with jealousy. How had she managed such a feat?

"It's easy. Just spit in the air and stand under it."

They erupted into laughter. The party had begun.

Käthe's words already slurred when she tucked Heidi into bed, taking a few moments to stroke her hair and kiss her forehead.

"Happy New Year, my kitten. By this time next year, the war will be over, and we will be so happy we will not even remember all this. It won't be long now."

The revelers got good and drunk, and Heidi lay there trying to drown out the sound of them having a raucous time celebrating the end of 1944.

Good riddance.

CHAPTER TEN

JANUARY THROUGH MARCH 1945: ZERO HOUR

AFTER KÄTHE SLEPT OFF HER New Year's Eve hangover, she went out for a while. Heidi remained in the apartment since it was not a nice day for playing outside. She wished again that she could find her *Max and Moritz* book to pass the time, and then she had an idea. Maybe she had left it in Tante Hedel's old bedroom before her mother blocked it off to save heat.

Her mother would be gone for a while, giving time to put everything back in place before her return. Heidi got to work shimmying the heavy wardrobe out of the way.

Heidi opened the door, and then she froze.

A skeleton of a man sat on the bed with saucer eyes and sunken cheeks. His head was shaved to stubble, and his skin was as gray as paper ash. He wore something like faded pajamas that had dingy stripes. His back hunched forward to prop elbows on his knees. Long, bony arms jutted from the sleeves while bones of fingers cupped around his face. He did not move when she opened the door, like his reflexes were gone. He did not speak, and his expression did not change. He just sat motionless, except for his eyes which raised toward hers. When they did, it gave her a chill like she gazed upon a ghost.

The ghost's eyes locked with hers—both he and she acknowledged that he had been seen.

Heidi stumbled backward through the door and closed it with trembling hands. She was putting the wardrobe back in place when her mother came through the door and spotted her there. Heidi jumped, and her body shook like it did when she awakened from one of her nightmares.

"Who is that man in the bedroom?"

The color drained from her mother's face, and she grasped Heidi's shoulders.

Her mother's words were urgent. "You saw nothing. There is nothing in there. You must never, ever speak of this. Not to anyone. Do you understand?"

Heidi nodded as she felt her mother's fingers digging into her skin so hard that it hurt. "I promise," she quivered.

Heidi was used to her mother's calm reassurance, and so the look in those blue, blue eyes frightened her. But even before Heidi saw the color drain from her mother's face, Heidi already knew she had just seen something terrible. That man's hollow expression was the most haunting thing she had seen yet in that awful war. What happened to him? Who had done that to him? And why was he in their apartment?

Heidi tiptoed from the room, leaving Käthe to inch the wardrobe back into place.

Heidi tiptoed from the room and an exhausted Käthe dragged a chair to the window, sank into it, and stared out.

Heidi could not hear Käthe whisper, "What have I done letting him stay here? But oh, God, what else could I do?"

Käthe could not tell Heidi that the man was Lizzie's boyfriend. She could not tell Heidi that he and others like him were why Käthe had been so needed in Berlin.

Käthe could not tell Heidi that after the opera and she started in the black market, her work had gradually shifted into the illicit trade of documents, information, and other acts of service for people whose lives were dependent on help. Her motivation had changed from necessity so she and

A Child In Berlin

Heidi could survive, to putting themselves in danger so others could. Every trade she made was an act of resistance. Käthe had accepted the risks because she could not live with herself if she stood idly by. She knew the cost of doing nothing. Especially, how could she turn away a friend when it had taken miracles for him to make it to her door?[1]

Käthe and Heidi could not speak any of that.

After that, Käthe's role-playing questions intensified.

A few days later, Jarda came for dinner. Heidi tried not to think about how someone else was in their apartment, hearing everything. *How long had the man been there?* She pushed the thought of the man from her mind. And she was good at doing that. Pushing fears and innumerable haunting images away had become an automatic habit. Heidi kept herself sane by focusing on whatever was in front of her.

Then she heard a knock, and a moment later, Jarda stood in front of her, holding something wrapped in paper. Good things came wrapped in paper.

---

1   We do not know how the man came to be in the back bedroom. Given that he was wearing striped pajamas, he must have come from a concentration camp. Historical records now show that there were people who escaped from camps, sometimes jumping from moving trains while being transported. Others managed to get away from the less closely guarded work sites around the city. Heidi remembered hearing her mother and others discuss Sachsenhausen, which was a concentration camp, although Heidi does not recall many details of those conversations. This camp outside Berlin would send workers to factories or supply labor in other ways. It is possible—although this is speculation—that the man got away from one of these assignments. Perhaps he crept through the city during a blackout and ended up in Käthe's home. It seems likely he had not been there long, or else wouldn't Käthe have scrounged up something else for him to wear? Heidi later learned that Käthe and Lizzie had been involved in helping him survive after he "took the plunge" into the underground. Jews hidden in Berlin were sometimes moved from place to place to avoid detection. Heidi remembers that the back bedroom had been closed off for quite some time, so she does not know if he or others had been there before, especially when Heidi had been sent to live elsewhere. Was this risk part of the reason Heidi was sent away? After the war, Heidi would fully understand the Holocaust and her mother's acts of selfless bravery. This knowledge had a profound impact on Heidi's sense of self, embracing her mother's example of doing what you believe is right and helping others even at great cost.

"I've brought a present for us," he said.

Käthe unwrapped a lump of fresh-looking, but unidentifiable, meat.

She accepted it gratefully, but she still raised an eyebrow and joked, "What is it, rat?"

He grinned and said, "No, they were all out of rat today. This is *ersatz* rat."

The three laughed.

"Rabbit," he said.

They all hoped that was true.

Käthe made a one-pot stew. They had a good time eating, talking, and laughing until the air raid sirens blared.

"Infernal noise," Käthe sighed.

Jarda pulled on his tweed coat with its fur collar as Heidi grabbed her always-packed suitcase.

They did not think it would be a bad bombing that night, so Jarda escorted them to the U-Bahn shelter entrance. Then he turned to leave, "I will go to the one near my place tonight."

Käthe protested, "It's too far; you won't make it."

But he would not relent. "We don't need gossip. You are a married woman."

People pushed around them, and the air raid warden barked at the laggards, "Move it, we need to secure the doors!"

Jarda nudged Käthe and Heidi toward the door and then backed away. There would be no changing his mind.

After they parted in different directions, Käthe spat, "Stupid man. He is going to the bar."

That night in the shelter, people held each other as the walls shook. The damage was close this time. Heidi nestled in rather than playing as she so often did. After a while, she glanced up to see that her mother's eyes were closed, and her lips moved almost imperceptibly in silent prayer.

On their way home, Heidi and her mother approached a corner where a bar had been only hours earlier. Now a crater had replaced it. Heidi shined her flashlight into the hole, and then she gasped. Käthe turned to look and spotted an arm bent and broken under the rubble. The arm was wearing a tweed coat with fur trim at the wrist. Jarda had taken his last drink.

Käthe wailed, and they hugged each other, weeping.

How did they make it back home that night? Neither one quite remembered walking, but once in the safety of their apartment, they crawled into bed together, mother and daughter crying until sleep came. Poor, poor Jarda.

Käthe returned to the crater the next day as workers in the area put out the remaining fires and looked for survivors. She identified Jarda's body, and then she went to the dentist's office where he worked to deliver the news. Together, she and the dentist worked out how to send word to his parents back home.

Käthe's emotions in the coming days cycled through anguish, rage, and guilt. She blamed herself with thoughts of, "if only." She was too overcome by sadness to think clearly. She should have been assigning guilt with the real villain: war itself and the people who made it.

Käthe's grief was so acute that it drained her of all energy. She did not bounce back this time, lying listless on the sofa or taking a nap in the afternoon. This was something Heidi had never seen her mother do, but this loss quite literally knocked her flat.

Käthe and Heidi had known too many losses for a full lifetime, let alone for a girl who was just shy of nine and a woman of only thirty.

■ ■ ■

One night later in January, they made their way home from a shelter, and Käthe walked straight into one of the fancy light poles designed by Hitler's architect, Albert Speer. It was the kind of light pole that children liked to climb because it had a series of narrow lips at the bottom, perfect for getting a foothold. Accidents like that should have eased up after so much blackout practice, but this was still a common mishap. Käthe's eyes had not adjusted to the dark night, and she was concentrating on looking at her footsteps when she ran into it right in front of her face.

The next day, Käthe was lying on the sofa. The run-in had left a nasty gash, and the bump to her head must have been worse than she realized because she would usually rub her temples with cologne. The thought of that made her queasy.

She lay there with her eyes closed and a wet towel on her forehead when an angry knock pounded on the door. Käthe bolted upright and the towel dropped into her lap.

"Open up!" The Gestapo had come.

This time it was not to ferret out some black-market goods or to slap her with a misdemeanor. They were coming for the skeleton man.

Heidi retreated to the window where she used to sit chubby-legged and waving to the passersby below. Being there made her feel like she had an exit as her mother opened the door.

The men stomped inside and began their search. They spotted the wardrobe right away. A moment later, they pushed it aside with such force that it toppled over sideways. They slammed open the bedroom door and dragged the man out, kicking him hard to get him moving. Then, they had had Käthe by the elbow, too. In an instant, they were leading her down the stairs. They did not bother searching the apartment for anything else; the men had their prize.

People came out of their apartments to watch, and Frau Pohl shouted, "Where are you taking her?"

"Moabit!"

Käthe called to Frau Pohl, "Please take care of Heidi until I return!"

Then, Käthe shouted to Heidi, "Stay here so I can find you when I get out."

Frau Pohl whisked Heidi to the apartment upstairs, where she spent the first two nights sleeping on a makeshift bed on the floor. Heidi was despondent at first, but she believed her mother would be back soon.

Meanwhile, Frau Pohl compared living situations and determined that Käthe's apartment was nicer than theirs, so Frau Pohl, the grandmother, and daughter decided to move downstairs.

It was what people in the city had been doing for years, moving whenever a home was destroyed, or a better apartment became available. Others, however, refused to leave their bombed-out homes. Instead, they set up camp inside partial ruins without windows, running water, or even walls.

At first, after Käthe was hauled away, Heidi could hardly breathe, replaying her mother's voice calling upon their neighbors to take care of her. Heidi was in knots about where her mother was being kept or what would happen. *How had the Gestapo found them out?* Heidi felt sick inside wondering if her mother thought that Heidi had told someone. After years of conditioning to keep her mouth shut and stay out of trouble, Heidi had kept her promise, but their worst fear had come true.

Heidi's recurring nightmare of her mother's coffin came more often now. She remembered her mother's words, "Life is at stake," and those words haunted her. *Whose life had she meant: the man's or theirs?*

Still, Heidi ferociously clung to the belief that her mother was alive and would return. *She would.*

Heidi was well-practiced at staying in the care of others, but she did not like how these people took over their apartment like it belonged to them. The women swatted at Heidi for spilling a cup of water and wasting it, but the next day Heidi's nose detected a foul odor. The little girl had pooped in a coffee cup and left it stinking in the kitchen. She was five years old, old enough to know better, but she was not punished. After the little boy had died, the girl could do no wrong, and the mother babied her. The unfair treatment grated at Heidi.

Then one day, Heidi noticed the woman put a piece of her mother's jewelry in her purse.

The woman brushed off Heidi's judging expression, "We need to eat."

Heidi was angry and said, "That is my mother's!"

The woman shrugged, "You think she is coming back?"

Heidi ran to the window blinking back tears. She peered out, looking hard at the ugly jail where her mother had been held before. She knew from asking around, and perhaps intuitively, that Käthe was not there this time. Moabit, where they had taken her, was a detention center that held people temporarily until sentencing. The female prisoners were then distributed to camps and prisons, not to the city jail. The city jail was for petty infractions, not for political crimes.

For the next few days, Heidi avoided Uschi and instead went for walks by herself so she could think. She stewed, turning over choices in her mind. She had already felt alone many times in her life. She thought, *I can make my way around town better than most grownups, even in the dark.*

Especially in the dark. I know where Mútti hid things, and I can trade. People will help me. I know who I can trust.

She felt a burning fury whenever she thought about the people living in her apartment. Heidi also believed it was only a matter of time before the women would pilfer everything.

She kicked a piece of rubble down the street and noticed a stray dog skulk out of the way. When she crouched down and called to it, the lonely dog came to her, sniffing and then licking her face, greedy for affection. After loving it for a while, she walked away. The dog followed her.

When Heidi brought it inside the apartment, the woman chastised her, "When we get back, if that mutt is still here, we will sell it as meat. We can't keep one more thing alive."

The women left Heidi for the ration lines. Heidi petted the dog for a long while. She had to make a choice before they returned, and then she experienced a singular moment of clarity.

She spoke aloud, "Mútti wanted someone to take care of me. No one else will do it but me."

Heidi gathered the women's belongings and dumped them outside the door. She closed the door satisfied, and then had an idea. She went back inside and retrieved the contaminated coffee cup, the one that the little girl had pooped in. Heidi placed it on top of the heap and arranged it *just so*, like a garnish on a plate of food.

"*There*," she said to herself. Her work was done.

Then she bolted the lock that could only open from the inside.

She heard them lumbering up the stairs, and her heart began pounding hard. First, they fumbled with the doorknob, then they thumped. Heidi's cheeks flushed hot with anger and defiance.

She shouted through the door, "I will take care of myself *and* my dog."

They shouted ugly words, hurled the apartment key at the door, and harrumphed back to their place.

Now Heidi was alone in the apartment, but she was comforted by the dog. It felt like he had been guided to her. They needed each other, and he gave her someone to talk to and someone to sleep alongside her. He made her feel like he was a guard at her door. The world was frightening outside, but the apartment walls were a cocoon inside.

Heidi had been left without her mother many times before, but there had always been adult overseers. They were responsible for food and for making all the decisions. Sometimes those decisions were to lasso her cat or kick out her dog. Some grownups poisoned children in the hospital, and some hauled her mother away.

She would make her own decisions from here.

In the previous months, Heidi had learned to scavenge with the boys, and she had always been able to get along with kind adults. Her mother had some food stored away, which would last longer now without more mouths eating it.

Heidi considered phoning cousin Agnes but then reasoned that she had better not. If she called Agnes, then her cousin would be there to retrieve her the same day. Heidi was done having someone else be in charge. Her mother had given instructions to stay there, and that is exactly what Heidi would do.

Heidi's heart ached with worry about her mother, but now she had to keep busy fending for herself. She spent the first days alone, opening every cubby where her mother may have stashed food or black-market goods. She kept valuable items hidden in place but cataloged where everything was. She got excited when she found the box of wall plaster. After fishing out the last precious egg, she cracked it into a pan. The smell made her recoil. When she tried giving it to her dog, he turned his nose up too. What a disappointment.

Heidi did not know how to cook meals, so most evenings, she would ration out a portion of dried peas, maybe a bottle of Fanta soda, or a vanilla sugar packet. Then she'd bring these upstairs to share with Uschi and her mother, who made them into something resembling a family meal.

Heidi learned that in famine times, there are people who invite others to the table, and there are those who steal. Heidi intuitively sensed who was who.

She did not give her dog a formal name, deciding instead to wait and name him together with the help of her mother. For now, she just called him *das hündchen*, "pooch."

Each day, Heidi kept to a routine that included standing in lines for water or for other rations and queuing up whenever she saw other adults doing so. Uschi usually kept her company, and they always brought the dog.

They were not roving the city with the neighborhood boys now. There was no school being held. People were just hunkering down inside their homes, holding their breath, and waiting. More families cleared out. Heidi only left the apartment empty when necessary because she wanted to guard it from looters, and in case her mother returned. The dog never left her side.

Air raid sirens blared every night now, and Heidi slept in her clothes to save time. She had to leave her dog each time, which made her ache.

She hated commanding him, "Stay here. It isn't safe for you out there."

Before heading out, she'd crack a window open and leave the door slightly ajar to prevent shattering. She wondered if her mother and the other people in prison went into shelters too, or was their whole building built like a bunker? She imagined it being built of thick concrete like the zoo tower and latched onto the idea that her mother would be safe inside a fortress.

One night after she returned from the shelter, her dog was not waiting for her. He must have been frightened and left through the door.

When he did not return, she thought, *Everyone leaves me.*

She somehow knew he was dead and chose to think a bomb had killed him instantly. It made the apartment seem much emptier, and an acute pang of loneliness stabbed at her in his absence. Heidi was too numb to cry that day; she just accepted it as another inevitable loss.

Would it have been better to never have met that dog, so she didn't hurt more now? *No.* She was glad that she had comforted the dog during the time they were together and to have made his time a little better. She had been glad of him, too. Nobody should have to be alone in the world. She was alone in the apartment now, but she still had her mother. She still had family in the village. There is a world of difference between *not here right now* and *gone forever.* She could wait.

The next night after her dog disappeared, sirens awoke her, but she could already hear planes getting close. She scrambled to put on her shoes and grabbed her suitcase. She headed to the window to open it a crack as she had been trained to do, but as she moved the blackout curtains aside, bright flashes of light illuminated her neighborhood. These were the Christmas trees that had once unhinged her mother.

She dove to the floor, curling into a ball and covering her head. The blast that followed was the biggest she had ever felt from above ground, and the closest to hit. A boom of pressure made her ears ring, and she could not hear herself screaming. She could not hear the tinkling of glass, but she felt bits of plaster falling onto her, almost as if time had slowed.

The building shook, heavy objects crashed to the floor, and the walls groaned under pressure—the whole building shimmied and heaved. Heidi gripped herself tighter, covering her head with her arms and waiting...waiting to see if she would still be alive when it was over.

Was this what it had felt like for Jarda in his coat and fur collar the night he had been killed? For her father? For her friend and their family killed in their sleep? Or did death come to everyone in a different way?

Then, almost as suddenly as it had begun, the planes turned tail, and the bombardment quieted. Heidi had on shoes because she had been preparing to go to the shelter, so she crept to the fancy bay windows. Glass crunched beneath her shoes from panes which lay in shards. The blackout curtains were tattered. A burning city illuminated her view. The moon was banished behind a blanket of swirling smoke that reflected red.

She glanced around the apartment and saw that the tile oven had come off the wall and lay broken on the floor. In addition, the front door was blown off its hinges. Now she saw the reason why they always left everything slightly ajar before going to the shelter.

She stood at the gaping window. The air should have been frigid, but the apartment across the street was burning. The whole façade was blown away, and she could see right into the apartment where Barry the St. Bernard had lived with his master and mistress. She remembered Frau Schüller dancing in front of that house once, almost manic in her relief to see it intact. But like so many others in this desolate city, the Schüllers had eventually retreated. Heidi was glad the woman would not have to witness this night or see Heidi peering directly into their beloved home.

It was like the whole building was a doll house where there is no front wall so children can play inside. The furniture was still arranged like it had been. In her mind, Heidi could envision Frau and Herr Schüller seated around the table with Barry at their side. The husband was reading his newspaper while finishing their morning rolls. Heidi could imagine moving each doll around the room, except now, flames ravenously licked from the back of the house. They curled around the sofa and melted the grandfather clock that Heidi had so loved.

A blast of air snapped Heidi out of an almost catatonic state, but the air was not cold like she might have expected from an early spring night. Instead, the gust carried heat from the blaze onto her cheeks. Ash fluttered from the sky like snow, coating the street white.

Heidi was awed by how quickly the fire had finished its work on the Schüller home, and then, just like that, there was nothing for them to come back to. Even if they survived the war, she somehow already knew she would never see them or Barry again.

Heidi had often seen destruction from a daylight vantage long after it was over. She thought she understood the power of these bombs, but to witness fire ravage everything in its reach was a degree of terror and awe that she could not have imagined. She was frozen, mesmerized in place as the world burned before her eyes.

Tears ran streaks through the soot on her cheeks.

Until this night, Heidi had absorbed the city's destruction with a brave face. Now her home was crumbling and exposed to the world, and something broke. Her eyes stung as she squinted out across the burning city. She began to sob like she had never done before, so afraid and alone was she. Her voice came out in desperate, guttural cries.

Then she found words, pleading, and repeating again and again, "I want my mútti. Please, God, send my mútti home. Please."

Her skinny body shook inside threadbare clothes as alternating waves of heat and bitter winter air blew in. Her whole body was crying.

Smoke stung her lungs, but still, her eyes fixated on the flames until they finally died and were replaced by the first low beams of daylight. Now exhausted and completely spent, she slumped away from the window. Through blurry vision, she found a blanket, curled into a ball underneath, and whimpered into the numbness of sleep. Hours later, Heidi awoke from numbness at the sound of a fire truck.

She was alive.

Sunlight should have been pouring through the open windows, but an orangish pea-soup haze clung to the city instead. Her lungs burned. She got herself up in haste and grabbed her water bucket. The fire truck was hours too late to quench the blaze; this was its regular drinking-water delivery. Filling her pail was a top priority as she desperately craved washing the soot from her face and eyes.

She was still dressed and in shoes, so she grabbed the bucket and ran.

When she returned to the apartment with a sloshing pail, she saw that Atlas was still holding the building on his shoulders, but everything was now off balance because there was nothing on either side to hold it up. The neighboring structures had been reduced to rubble, but somehow their building still stood. It looked forlorn and precarious, but the one building where Heidi had been had held. She still had a home, still had a place where her mother could find her.

In the apartment, Heidi kept most of the water for drinking but ladled some into a basin. She splashed a little onto her eyes to flush the smoke. Then she dabbed a rag into it and scrubbed at the soot on her cheeks. She didn't want to look like a street urchin when her mother returned.

Next, she shook glass from the tablecloth, turning her face away from flying shards. She swept glass from the floor and tacked the blackout curtains as firmly as she could to keep the cold at bay. Finally, she propped the door against the frame. It would offer no safety, but it helped her *feel* more secure to not have a gaping hole where the door should be. The door marked her space. Visitors were not welcome to come trouncing in.

Uschi and her mother checked in on her; they were still alive too. Uschi's mother looked like a frightened mouse.

Uschi looked tired but tried to cut the tension, "That was some show we got last night. Front row seats."

Heidi quipped back, "We didn't even have to pay to get in."

Heidi had cleared most of the glass by dinnertime, and it was time to rest. She retrieved what was left of her bread from a cabinet and opened a can of milk. She sopped bread into the milk and scooped a cup of water from the pail and drank heartily.

It had been a day of hard work, and she felt satisfied with what she had accomplished. She had channeled her energy into sweeping and cleaning, and the effort kept her mind from thinking.

But now that nightfall had come, she carefully washed her hands and then scrubbed her face again until she was satisfied there was no soot left. Then, went to the suitcase that she had hidden from the Gestapo, the one with the fabric and curtains. She opened it and moved the white curtains aside—the ones that had been removed from service on the first day of the war. The fabric was gone now; instead, she found her mother's summer clothes. Heidi buried her face in them, losing herself in Käthe's scent.

Each day after that, she did a little more to restore order to her apartment, and the act breathed hope into her soul. She did not allow herself to open the trunk very often for fear the scent would be lost forever, but it was an occasional reward after a tiring day.

Heidi created and clung to her routines, and days passed into weeks. Then, finally, spring began to warm the city, and the apartment was not so frigid now.

Heidi's ninth birthday was March 12, and she rummaged through her mother's goods. The best she had left was some brown beet sugar. She took it to Uschi's mother, who readily accepted it and invited her for a meal. She was happy to be with people, but she did not tell them it was her birthday. She couldn't bear their pity, which might make her cry.

After Heidi had locked the neighbors out, she started going to mass by herself. One Sunday, they invited her to receive her first communion with a group of other children to be held on April 15.[2]

Heidi believed her mother would be pleased, and was certain that Oma would be, but her heart ached at the thought of having this important day without her mother or any other family there. There would be no white dress, no relatives coming, and no celebration at home. At any other time, Heidi surely would have waited for her mother's

---

2 On that same day, Hitler issued a decree to be disseminated to soldiers fighting in the east, which said, in part, "Anyone ordering you to retreat, unless you know him well, is to be taken prisoner at once and if necessary, killed on the spot, no matter what his rank may be." It was intended that German soldiers fight to the death. Source: Cornelius Ryan, *The Last Battle: The Classic History of the Battle of Berlin* (New York, NY: Simon & Schuster), 347–348.

return. But Heidi was also bargaining. It was a time of begging God to protect her mother. After so much pleading, if God asked this one thing of her now, how could she refuse?[3]

But in the end, whether she wanted to admit it or not, it may have been a more basic need that made her decide to receive her first communion. Hunger. Heidi would have to attend catechism classes at someone's home, and they might offer her something to eat.

It turned out that Heidi was right. After the first lesson, the family whose apartment held the class asked her to share

---

[3] What Heidi and other Berliners could not know was that Hitler's generals were also bargaining. By all accounts, they knew the war was lost and it was time to plan an orderly retreat and surrender to save as many lives as possible. They needed to evacuate Berlin before it was overtaken, which now was not a matter of if but when. They had been telling the people that Berlin was the best defended city in Europe, which was probably true when it came to an air war, but they had never considered the possibility that ground troops would ever reach the city. Their troops were now deployed elsewhere, leaving the capital city virtually defenseless on the ground. It was a city of women, children, and the elderly. Anyone who could have been conscripted to fight had already been taken for duty on other fronts. Not until March was the city's defense given any real consideration, and by that time it was far too late. Now, the generals strategized among themselves and decided it was time to confront Hitler with the truth. In early April, the generals made their way to Hitler's bunker beneath the Reichstag, which was only a few kilometers from Heidi's neighborhood in Alexanderplatz. When the generals arrived, they found Hitler as ruined as the city. His hands trembled and his eyes looked wild. The operations chief, Colonel Hans-Georg Eismann, later said, "His entire body trembled.... His hands, in which he was holding some pencils, flew wildly up and down, the pencils beating on the arms of the chair in the process. He gave the impression of being mentally deranged. It was all so unreal—especially the thought that an entire people lay in the hands of this human ruin." In that meeting, General Gotthard Heinrici said, "My Führer, the fact is that, at best, we can hold out for just a few days. Then, it must all come to an end." There was dead silence. But Hitler rallied his own faculties and instead of accepting the reality before them, spun a vision of last-minute miracles. He had his generals in his palm again, and instead of planning an evacuation or retreat, the generals gambled the lives of their men and civilians for last-ditch fighting to hold out longer. Heinrici continued to press for a retreat, saying, "I tell *you*, all these men will be slaughtered at the front! Slaughtered!" It would only buy them days, but the country would pay a heavy price in human life. As they left the conference room, General Heinrici repeated softly to himself, "It's all for nothing. All for nothing." Source: Ryan, *The Last Battle*, 255–265.

a meal. Over dinner, they also suggested that she should stay with them.

It wasn't the first time someone had encouraged her to stay with them, especially if they needed a babysitter for younger children or if they thought she could help in another way. But the tone of this family seemed concerned for her welfare, and she appreciated the sentiment. As rumors grew that the Russians were closing in, it was time for people to gather and protect each other.[4]

But Heidi shook her head just as she had whenever she had been asked before.

"Thank you, but I need to keep the apartment for when my mother returns. I promised I would stay put."

The family looked at her with weary eyes. They implored again for her to stay with them.

The mother could not help herself from adding, "My dear, what if she does not come back?"

Maybe the mother felt it was best to prepare Heidi for the inevitable, but her defeated eyes made Heidi angry, and she fought back inside.

Heidi stood her ground, "She *is* coming."

Under normal circumstances, this family might have insisted that she stay, but everybody had problems. Besides, who were they to say what anyone else should do? So, they let the girl go.

---

4   On March 19, Hitler issued a decree ordering the destruction of German infrastructure to prevent its use by Allied forces. It was officially titled "Decree Concerning Demolitions in the Reich Territory." Speer was put in charge of carrying it out, an order that he deliberately failed to obey. He was one of the few advisors willing to confront Hitler, and had done so months earlier, telling him the war was lost. Speer believed they should make plans for retreat to preserve as much of the country as possible. He saw ahead to his own responsibility for rebuilding. Hitler flew into a rage, saying, in essence, that if the war was lost, the people were unworthy, that there was nothing to live for anyway, and that scorched earth would be their course. General Dietrich von Choltitz had similarly refused to carry out a direct order by Hitler to destroy Paris before it was liberated by the west.

As Heidi trudged home, she thought about how this family had responded with pity, which made Heidi rebel. Sometimes, however, people over-compensated with fake optimism, trying to make her feel better. When they did, Heidi remembered her mother saying, "If it's perfect, it is fake."

And so, it was worse when people projected false brightness. Something in their voices smacked of desperation, of telling themselves lies. This caused Heidi's mood to swing the other way, and some color faded from her hope at those times.

Regardless, Heidi clung to her resolve. She had no control over whatever was happening outside, so she now stayed inside the walls of her apartment as much as possible. It was her space, and she kept it ready for her mother's return.

Heidi now felt resigned to being in Berlin regardless of which country got there first. Even if her mother got out soon, they would never make it to Stuttgart so near the end.

Longer stretches would go by during that time without Heidi and Uschi seeing each other. Uschi and her mother were drawing close like most families were.

April 13 was a day Heidi did not go out but sat on the sofa thinking about her first communion. Would it still happen, or would the fighting be too close by then? She had been instructed that they would still proceed with the ceremony as planned unless there was war in the streets. The congregation felt that they needed their rites at this time more than any other.

As Heidi mindlessly thumbed through a book she had read a hundred times, she heard footsteps on the stairs. The building was mostly empty by then. Who could be coming?

Her heart pounded, and her cheeks flushed. She crouched along the wall next to where the door was propped in the opening. She always kept a frying pan and a broom there in case she needed to use them as weapons against an intruder.

Then, finally, she heard the person stop. There was no knock. Turning the knob wouldn't do any good. Whoever was there could just push the door aside to enter at will. Instead, she saw a woman's hands grasp the door to gently slide it out of the way. Heidi peered up through the crack and gasped, "Mútti!"

CHAPTER ELEVEN

APRIL THROUGH DECEMBER 1945: THE AFTERMATH

Heidi sprang up and startled her mother, and they knocked the door to the floor. Heidi rushed into her mother's arms. Then, after a long embrace, they parted to look at one another. Käthe was bone-thin and dust-streaked, but her eyes gleamed.

They fell again into each other's arms, hugging with the exuberance of young children. It was real. Her mother had come home.

Before this moment, neither had allowed herself to acknowledge the presence of fears looming like a specter over them.

Now, all the unnamed fear vaporized. It felt like a gust of happiness whisked every demon from the room.

In this world, there could be no sadder moment than when a child is torn from her mother, and the opposite is also true. Joy was too small a word to describe the reunification of Heidi and Käthe on that day. They had already experienced that agony followed by torturous waiting and indescribable longing. Now that Käthe and Heidi were back in each other's arms, everything lost was restored. Every color of light burst from their two hearts.

That moment was a singular experience that neither would repeat again in their lifetimes. There are simply no words to describe a reunion like theirs.

They wanted to tell each other everything at once, but Käthe staggered like she only had the strength to walk from the doorway to the bed. She beckoned Heidi to lie down, saying, "Come here, little mouse. I am exhausted. Let's hold each other." Heidi fetched some water for Käthe to drink, and she dampened a rag to wipe Käthe's face. Käthe's weakened limbs sank into the bed like they might never move again. Heidi listened to her mother's heartbeat until she also fell into a nap—neither one had slept so securely since January.

When Käthe awoke, she said, "Today, the guards walked in and told me my sentence was up. Just like that, they let me walk home. The women's prison on Barnimstrasse is not too far from here."

When Käthe said the word "home," it caught Heidi off guard, releasing a flood of emotion. Now with her mother back, she had a home again. Heidi had guarded the space for her mother's return, but it had only felt like a shelter in Käthe's absence. Heidi had taken pride in the apartment, but home is where you are loved.

Heidi then told how she had locked out the others and saved her mother's things.

Käthe glanced around at the crumbling apartment and then into her daughter's black-cherry eyes—eyes that were wise beyond her years. Heidi was already so old, so young.

Käthe said, "You are the bravest person I have ever known."

Heidi looked back at her mother and smiled a dimpled smile. At once, she looked like a child again.

Heidi said, "I knew you were coming back."

They lay there curled up together and smelled the familiar warmth of each other's bodies. Käthe smelled as wonderful as she always had; she was simply one of those people with a naturally pleasant scent, and Heidi nuzzled into her.

Then, as the grogginess of the nap wore off, Käthe smiled and said, "I have exciting news. Are you ready?"

Heidi believed she was ready for anything.

"I am going to have a baby. You will be a big sister!"

This idea thrilled Heidi, and then she blurted, "Who is the father?"

Käthe winced at her daughter's bluntness. It would never have occurred to Käthe at Heidi's age to ask such a question. Käthe smiled and said, "Richard, of course. My husband."

Käthe wanted Heidi to fully understand the words that followed. "This baby is a miracle. When they put me in prison,[1] I was morning sick. Because of my condition, they took me out of the regular quarters and into the infirmary. I got better food, and they were kind to me there."

Being pregnant and sick may have saved her life. Maybe they also had pity on a mother whose daughter would be orphaned if she died. The whole reason that Käthe was spared the worst may never be known. But, whatever the reason, it is likely that she used every resource she had to negotiate for her life. She could have been sentenced to die, but they sent her for better care instead.[2]

---

[1] We cannot be certain where Käthe was held because she did not speak of her ordeal in front of Heidi. Heidi remembered Käthe saying they were taking her to Moabit when the Gestapo hauled her away. Moabit was a sentencing facility that generally only held prisoners temporarily. Heidi knew (but does not recall how she knew) that her mother was not being held at the jail at Alexanderplatz. From the fragments we do know, we have surmised it likely that she was held at the Central Berlin Women's prison, which was located north of Alexanderplatz, on the Barnimstrasse in Friedrichshain. It operated between 1868 and 1974. There were many political prisoners, including Rosa Luxemburg, who was probably the most prominent. We also know that they set Käthe free as the Russians closed in on the city, and she walked home after that. So, she couldn't have been in a concentration camp outside the city. There would have been no way to get back to central Berlin during the chaos of those final days.

[2] Suicide was common among inmates as it was in the general population. One friend she made in prison experienced such despair that she jumped from a window to commit suicide, only to survive with two broken legs. She and Käthe became lifelong friends after that. A seamstress by trade, the woman made many of Käthe's and Heidi's dresses after the war.

Heidi admired her mother's bump. It showed because Käthe was so malnourished.

Heidi asked her mother, "Does Richard know?"

Käthe answered, "No. I couldn't send mail and wouldn't have known where to send it anyway. Now, I pray he survives to be a father."

That night they crawled into the same bed again and said words they would repeat many times. "If we die now, we will die together."

With fighting drawing so close, they might have been restless and unsettled, but the two slept more soundly in each other's arms than ever before.

When they awoke, Heidi remembered to tell her mother, "My first communion is tomorrow. So, you made it back in time…." Then she stopped short before finishing her thought.

Käthe pressed her. "What is it, little mouse?"

"I wanted you to be there. I didn't know if I should do it without you, but I thought maybe God would bring you home."

Her mother kissed the top of her head. "You have grown up on me."

Then Käthe knitted her brow. "What will you wear?"

Heidi retrieved her air raid suitcase and unfolded the perfectly preserved dress and patent leather shoes she had been storing. But when she held the dress up, Käthe frowned.

Heidi saw her mother's look and said, "They told me I don't have to wear white."

Käthe shook her head. "It's not the color. When was the last time you wore that outfit?"

Heidi shrugged, and Käthe urged her to try it on.

Every night when the sirens blared, she had been lugging a suitcase with a pristine outfit that she had long since outgrown.

Heidi's face fell. "I was keeping that dress nice until I had a reason to wear it. Everything I own looks like it would be worn by Der Struwwelpeter."

Käthe's eyes darted around the apartment for inspiration. She had an idea when she spotted the blown-out window and its blackout blanket.

Käthe went to the trunk where she had been storing her white curtains since the first day of the war in 1939, a lifetime ago. These curtains reminded her of fresh snow blanketing a grimy city. Käthe had deposited those curtains into a suitcase like she was awaiting a ticket into peacetime. It was almost over now. The curtains had been preserved all these years, even from the Gestapo, for precisely this moment.

Käthe took Heidi's measurements. The girl had not grown in height, but she thought it again; *Heidi looked older—far beyond her years.*

Käthe spread the fabric, drew a pattern, and sharpened her good shears. Then she went to work. She focused all day, stopping only to take inventory of their food. Heidi had saved some salt and dried peas, so Käthe got these soaking for soup.

Käthe noticed how Heidi seemed constantly alert to sounds outside the apartment. Her instincts had sharpened while being alone.

Käthe sent Heidi to bed and stayed up much of the night working until she had completed the dress.

The next day Käthe brushed Heidi's hair as emotion spilled from her eyes, "I am proud of you."

At this, Heidi peered at her mother as though she had something important to say that had been bottled up.

"What is wrong, my treasure?"

Heidi tried to hold back, but tears came anyway as she blurted out, "It wasn't me—I didn't tell anyone about the man in our apartment. I kept the secret."

Käthe wrapped her arms around the girl and consoled her, "I know. They told me in prison that someone reported me."

Heidi now felt free from a burden that had worried her for so long.

Mother and daughter held hands as they walked, unwilling to let each other go. Heidi's bright white dress looked dazzling in contrast to the bombed-out world. She felt light, pretty, and happy beyond measure. She received her first communion rite, witnessed by her mother. The priest acknowledged the miracle of Käthe's return, adding a feeling of celebration and hope in the face of whatever lay ahead.

They had long grown accustomed to feeling unsettled, realizing that each time they parted with friends could be the last time to ever see them. However, this goodbye was even more poignant. No one could foresee the future, not even for a few days.

They went home that afternoon, and Käthe slept until morning.

The next day after communion, Heidi and Käthe tried to put the apartment back together, but after some effort, Käthe surveyed their work. The kachelofen was a heap of rubble. Some shards of glass had still escaped the cleanup effort. The windows were all out. Käthe led Heidi outside to look at the building from that vantage, and they assessed the odds of it standing if another bomb dropped in the area. Käthe predicted it would topple.

After climbing the stairs, she paused at the threshold. They did not have the hardware to hang the door that leaned against the frame. It would not close properly, let alone lock. The Americans had stopped bombing, leaving the city's demise to a horde of Russians. She shuddered.

It was not safe to stay there. Remarkably, the city's telephone lines still worked, so Käthe phoned cousin Agnes.

The women agreed they would all be safer banding together. So they prepared to leave for Hohenschönhausen.

Käthe laid out two sets of clothes and began sewing her jewelry into the linings. They would wear the extra layer and carry other valuables in suitcases. Getting caught with the shortwave radio was too much of a risk, so Käthe traded it for food. What a painful decision. They knew how starved they would be for information in the days and weeks to come.

Heidi said her goodbyes to Uschi. Her eyes welled. "What if I never see you again?"

Uschi said, "What are you talking about? We will find each other no matter what. Sisters forever. Promise?"

Heidi embraced Uschi. "Promise. I will be back before you know it. So, save your movie money."

"Too bad the theaters are all bombed."

Uschi's mother came to the door and said, "May God bless and keep you, Heidi."

Heidi and her mother were already outside on the street when Käthe remembered something that Agnes had said on their visit months earlier. The two trudged back up and set down their things.

Her mother found the red fabric she had been saving for a dress. She retrieved her good sewing scissors from the suitcase and cut the fabric into two large rectangles. She then pinned one as an additional layer underneath each of their dresses. It reminded Heidi of how her Oma had worn several layers of skirts with an apron on top.

Käthe's plan was to hem the edges once they got to Agnes's place to wear as shawls as a signal of solidarity with the Russians.

With that task complete, Heidi and her mother left gain. They picked their way through bombed-out streets to Agnes's apartment. When Agnes opened the door, she gave her cousin a long hug of love and relief. They were comforted to be all together now.

Shortly after they arrived, air raid bombings stopped altogether, and there was a deep quiet that felt ominous. Then, on April 19, the smell of baking bread wafted through the neighborhood. The baker had used up his stockpiles and was giving bread to anyone in line. People started grabbing it from each other's hands until he came out waving a huge spatula as if to swat people if they did not stop behaving like heathens.

April 20 was Hitler's birthday, and the sky was rust-red. The city lay eerily quiet. No trains entered or left the city, and very few cars. Telegraph and mail service had stopped. Barricades were going up everywhere to slow the advance of Russians, but people were passing along a new joke. "How long will it take for the Soviets to break through the barricades? Nine minutes laughing their heads off, and one minute to blast them to oblivion."

Some people whispered another sobering quip, "I hope you enjoyed the war, because the peace is going to be terrible."

Everyone knew that Russian revenge was coming. A new rumbling sound came from outside the city's S-Bahn ring. It was not from air bombing but from ground fighting outside "fortress Berlin." People had hoped it would be the Americans because word had traveled throughout Europe that when the Americans took over an area, they brought celebrations, peace, and supplies. But this was the Russians.

People feared that this conquering army would be unleashed like dogs with one goal: to exact revenge on the capital.

For years, Berliners had been told that their city was impenetrable, but the truth was that Hitler and his generals had never planned for ground troops to get that far. So now, it was a city of women and children, and it lay virtually defenseless. There was no real plan for their protection or evacuation.

Instead of the usual party for Hitler's birthday, people were burning their Nazi flags and party badges. Old soldiers and young boys were being conscripted into a last-ditch militia.

A few people posted sardonic signs recalling the words of previous birthday celebrations, "For all this, we thank the Führer."

The next day still brought no overhead bombings, and Heidi longed to see how Uschi was doing, so she phoned her friend.[3] They arranged to meet at a park halfway between them, a walk of about five kilometers for each girl. Heidi had played grownup for so long that when the girls met in the park, she ran around in carefree delight. Heidi reveled in the feeling of exercising her muscles and swinging on the monkey bars. The number of children swelled as they came out to enjoy a break. The sound of children squealing in the park carried through the quiet air, and people opened their windows. Children chased each other in a massive game of tag.

Then, an older boy stopped cold and held up a hand. The others froze. Then, they heard—or rather, felt—something like thunder in the distance. There was a low vibration and a sudden change in the air.

Planes were on the way. A lot of planes.

Heidi went pale, realizing how far she was from Agnes's apartment. Heidi, Uschi, and the other children scattered in every direction, hoping to outpace whatever was coming.

---

[3] Telephone service remained operational throughout the time when the Red Army took over Berlin.

Within a minute or two, Heidi could make out the familiar rattle of Russian planes. Every person outside was now on a dead run, but they were quickly overtaken by planes overhead. The park's flak tower began shooting at the aircraft flying lower to the ground than Heidi had ever seen. They were shooting everywhere, especially at the tops of buildings. Bullets ricocheted, windowpanes flew out, and debris fell all around.

Up ahead, Heidi saw a man stagger, and blood pooled around him. As she passed, her peripheral vision caught the sight of him holding his guts before he dropped to his knees and then fell face forward. At first, Heidi ran close to the buildings for cover from the plane gunners overhead but then had to dodge falling roof rubble. She shielded her head while running. Nowhere was safe.

Then, she spotted people ducking inside a brewery, and Heidi followed them. The tall vats were likely to hold up and offer some protection, so she crouched next to one. She noticed others in there, and now there was nothing to do but wait.

In Heidi's young life, she had felt anxious, bewildered, lonely, or sad, but seldom truly afraid. Her mother generally kept her cool, and Heidi's emotions followed this lead. But here in the brewery,[4] with bedraggled people huddling and waiting, a palpable feeling of fear billowed out from them, and they pulled Heidi into their panic.

She gripped her knees to stop the trembling and then heard a voice.

"Heidi!"

---

[4] We suspect the brewery she entered was the Schultheiss Brewery in Hohenschönhausen. It is in the right neighborhood and was in operation at the time. See David McCormack, *The Berlin 1945 Battlefield Guide: Part 2 – The Battle of Berlin* (UK: Fonthill Media, 2017), 140–141.

She looked up and recognized a teenage boy who lived across the courtyard from Agnes. He sat with a friend, and she recognized them both. They were good boys, and they motioned for her to come over. She gladly did so.

One boy asked, "Are you alone here?"

She nodded, and he responded, "Stick with us now."

It was a great comfort to be in the presence of these boys, who were so strong and protective. With all the men away, boys like them had risen to the occasion, filling in gaps of manhood in every way they could. They were too young to be drafted, so they carried the burdens their fathers had to leave.

The three waited and waited some more. Heidi's mind was frozen on an image of her mútti, as though she could feel Käthe's panic from across the city. Käthe had not known she was leaving to meet Uschi.

One of the boys spoke what Heidi was thinking for all of them, "Your mother must be worried sick."

Heidi's big eyes welled up with tears. Their families would be anxious, too. They all felt the agony of uncertainty: who was okay and who was not? They could never know until they got home.

All the while, the rumbling they felt from the ground got louder and louder. Finally, one of the boys spoke.

"I can't stand this waiting. Should we make a run for it?"

The second boy and Heidi stood up without debating. The three crept to the door and poked their heads out into the dusty haze that obscured the sun. It gave them a feeling of cover. One boy grabbed each of Heidi's hands and took off in a dead run. The boys had such athletic legs that Heidi could not keep up. Their work-hardened bodies were fueled with adrenaline, and they did not slow down or leave the girl behind. Instead, they tightened their grips and lifted her feet off the ground. The sound of gunfire and explosions blurred out of focus as instinct helped them pick the safest path forward.

The boys' bodies were driving forward in a rhythm of running legs, pounding blood, and hard breathing. They did not stop and did not look around until their building came into view. Then, a final push of energy catapulted them forward until they dove headlong through the door of the boys' apartment. They collapsed into a heaving mass at the base of the stairs.

It took a few minutes for the three to rise, leaving the damp prints of their bodies in a film of dust on the floor. Drips of sweat had streaked lines through the grime on their faces. When the boys walked through their doors to their homes, they had the look of soldiers returning from battle.

Heidi went through the courtyard and fell into her mother's embrace. The poor woman was hysterical. It was only the second time Heidi remembered seeing absolute terror on her mother's face. Heidi and her mother then went into the wash kitchen adjacent to the main part of the house where they had been sleeping at night. Now, there was nothing more to do but wait and feel the ground vibrate with increasing intensity. The tanks were getting closer.

Time blurred while Russian tanks took over their part of the city. Hohenschönhausen was one of the first neighborhoods to capitulate to the Red Army on the evening of April 21. Before it fell, people had the same idea as Agnes. They draped any red cloth they owned from inside their windows.

Shortly after their neighborhood succumbed, an officer came around to speak to the people, and Käthe went out to hear what he had to say. He had a German translator, but Käthe could get by with some Russian mixed with Polish to communicate. It was a savvy move not to speak German.

The officer told them they were there to liberate the city from Hitler and that they would be okay if they did not fight back. However, he also confided a warning to them.

"The first wave of soldiers with me are professionals, and we believe in honor. But the ones that follow can be brutes. So be careful and stay inside, especially until military order is established."

And so, he confirmed the rumors they had been hearing. After that, everyone burrowed into their homes as securely as possible until it ended.

There were still some Nazi loyalists hiding in the rubble, so isolated gunfights would erupt. If the Russians caught any alive, they'd hold a public hanging, forcing people outside at gunpoint to watch. Heidi was never made to look, but she got what was happening from afar.

One day, Heidi heard a Hitler Youth outside loudly yelling, "Heil Hitler" at a Russian soldier. She did not see but heard the soldier beating the boy. Then, finally, it was quiet again.

By April 25, there were Russian ground troops everywhere. The streets were quiet late at night between May 1 and 2 when Heidi and her mother were awakened by the sound of a teenage boy who was shouting in the street.

"Hitler is dead! The son of a bitch is dead!"

Heidi pulled a curtain back to see it was one of the boys who had helped her in the brewery. She later learned that the Russians had recruited them to walk to the Reichstag to see what was happening. They returned with a report that they had seen the red flag flying over the building and got confirmation that Hitler was dead.

The next day, they all learned that a ceasefire had been struck. They later understood that Hitler had killed himself in his bunker with his wife of less than a day, Eva Braun. Among the suicides were Joseph and Magda Goebbels, who had also poisoned their children. In addition, the fascist Italian dictator Benito Mussolini was executed on April 28.

On May 2, people spilled out onto the streets for the first time in what seemed like ages, talking, and embracing. They basked in a feeling of "it's over" while wondering their fate, "now what?"

As far as Heidi could tell, nobody danced on any tables.

Shortly after the ceasefire, Heidi awoke to a horse neighing outside. She ran to the window and opened it to see. Horses pulled a large wagon that held a field kitchen, and they stopped to set up in front of Agnes's building. The horses were sweaty, and a breeze carried the smell of their damp bodies and droppings to Heidi's nose.

In an instant, her soul alighted, returning to thoughts of the countryside where she had felt expansive and free. She suddenly yearned for the crunch of snow in the moonlight and the scurrying sounds of creatures in the trees.

Heidi found that the soldiers in their courtyard were not terrifying. For one thing, they brought food.

The smell of their supper wafted through the neighborhood, and children came out to beg. They gathered around, and the soldiers just shooed them away. Heidi could not resist going down, and then she hollered up to her watchful mother, "Throw me a spoon." Her mother wrapped one in paper and dropped it down. Heidi then walked up to the line with her head high wearing a grin so wide the soldiers made room for her, laughing at her moxie. When her turn came to the man dishing out rations, she looked up with that beaming, dimpled smile and held out her spoon. Her infectious charm caught him off guard, and he began to laugh, scooped goulash into a tin, then placed it in the girl's hands.

Käthe was relieved more than she could express to see how kind the Russian soldiers generally were toward children. At nine years old and skinny, Heidi looked young for her age, too small to be a target of the marauding soldiers who came out after dark demanding schnapps, watches, and women. Before evening everyone would retreat indoors and do their best to protect the wives and daughters, sometimes even grandmothers. It was perilous at night, but young women were not safe any time of day.

The enormity of these ravages would last a lifetime—but too often, those lifetimes were cut short. Abortions and suicides were rampant, and many died from injuries. The most common topic for weeks had been suicide—those who took cyanide out of fear before Berlin fell and the women who jumped from bridges after being raped. One broken mother wrapped her children around her waist with a rope and leaped into a water tank. She drowned them all, contaminating the water for everyone else.

Some families created hiding spaces for their girls under the floorboards, and others rubbed their skin with wood stains to look ugly. Some disguised themselves as young men.

Desperation also drove some women to form relationships with the soldiers. It was better to *give* than have it *taken*, and these quasi-consensual relationships brought food, supplies, and protection. This became an increasingly common arrangement in Agnes's neighborhood. However, the prevalence of it made Käthe uneasy, and she hoped that being pregnant would afford her some sympathy.

When Käthe sensed they had worn out their welcome with Agnes, they decided it was time to test the waters back in Alexanderplatz. With the bombing stopped, their building should hold, and warmer weather meant the missing glass would not be such an inconvenience. Also, they wanted to be there in case news came about Richard. Did he survive?

After the ten-kilometer walk, they arrived to find their lonesome building still there. Atlas still held a wobbly world on his shoulders.

Heidi ran upstairs to see Uschi. But they were not there. There was no note or other instructions, and Heidi's heart sank with disappointment and worry. Would they be back soon? She and Uschi had promised they would be sisters no matter what and to find each other when it was over. Heidi vowed to keep her promise.

The next day, Heidi began venturing out to see what had survived and who was still around. The Alexanderplatz neighborhood was all but obliterated, and she had frequent flashbacks of the man and his guts and the sound of gunfire raining around her.

She kept her eyes trained on the ground and tried to avoid gruesome sights. But at the U-Bahn entrance near their apartment, she saw that a tank had fallen halfway into a sinkhole with its gun tipped downward. As she walked around, her eye spotted something glinting in the sun, and she could not look away. Her vision panned out and then she noticed a body lying beside the tank. It was partially pinned underneath it, dead and black. She had seen a lot of bodies by then, and she usually looked around or through them—never directly at a corpse. But this was a girl turned half sideways with her face away. From behind, however, Heidi could see red hair clumped and matted with blood. One arm extended out ahead and there was a ring on one of the bloated fingers. Heidi realized that it was the ring that had caught her eye, a blue gemstone sparkling in a dreary world. She stared at it, but it took her mind some to process what she saw.

The stone was the color of Uschi's eyes.

The world slowed, and her vision blurred as realization dawned on her.

Heidi dropped to her knees and vomited violently before staggering home to her mother.

Käthe held Heidi and the two wept bitter tears like they had done for so many others lost. Every new heartbreak had been the worst one yet, and this was Heidi's worst of all.

Heidi would carry an unspoken grief over Uschi for a lifetime, for it was too sharp, too unjust, and too sacred a thing to dull with words. The senseless tragedy of it would never leave her. Not ever.

■ ■ ■

A contingent of Russian soldiers was assigned to the area, so before Käthe decided to remain there, she tracked down the officer in charge and negotiated protection for them. She still had resources, and this was the time for their use.

But one evening, a drunken soldier staggered up the stairs. A few minutes later, and they could hear Frau Pohl screaming. Not satisfied with just one, he thirsted for more and stumbled down the steps, kicking down their unhung door and stumbling into their room.

Heidi and Käthe were together, and the soldier fell onto them, drunk out of his wits. The two kicked and struggled as he groped at them, trying to get hold.

Somehow in all the jostling, his gun fired into the wall. The sound spooked him to his feet, and he stumbled away.

It was a very close call.

The next day, Käthe reported it to the officer in charge, and she described the savage man. He was dragged into the street and severely beaten. One of the men hit him with a pole until he fell to the ground with blood dripping down his face.

Käthe and Heidi noticed that there seemed to be two kinds of Russian soldiers. The first were the ones most remembered by Germans later—the ones so hardened by war and seeking revenge that they were capable of atrocities. The others were from small villages and wore such naïve innocence they were almost childlike. They had shy, good-natured smiles and seemed incapable of hurting anyone.

Käthe and her friends snickered when one story circulated about a Russian soldier who was seen cooking potatoes in a metal bedpan, not knowing what it was for.

By this time, Käthe was five months pregnant and anemic from lack of food, so Heidi ventured out to forage. Everyone was starving, and one early act by the Russians was to break down the doors of any remaining stores so the citizenry could loot. People grabbed what they could, often obtaining mismatched shoes and clothes that did not fit. People then traded what they found for anything else they might use.

One day, Heidi was out exploring, and she saw some people breaking down a set of wide gates set into a high berm that led into a cave-like structure. She followed the frenzy into a cavern where cheese from the mountains lay aging on shelves.

By then, people were leaving with all the spoils, but it was cool inside, and she liked the smell of stone and earth. She wanted to stay longer to explore, even if the food was gone.

Then, a hissing noise started coming from the pipes above, and the adults scattered like rats. Everyone was on high alert those days and easily frightened by anything that looked or sounded unusual. They had been horrified to hear rumors that people had drowned inside a flooded U-Bahn station during the last days of fighting, and there was rampant speculation that Hitler had killed these people to clear them out.

When people were spooked, Heidi had learned all too well that one of the greatest dangers was getting trampled. So rather than running with the crowd, she pulled herself up just like she did on monkey bars. From there, Heidi crouched out of the way and let the mob disperse. From that vantage point, she spotted a massive wheel of cheese with wax skin pushed way back into a corner. She climbed even higher to get it but was approaching closer and closer to the hissing. Her heart was pounding, but she did not care. This much food was irresistible.

Then, as suddenly as the sound had begun, it stopped. She exhaled relief as her brain kicked into gear: the sound was just part of the ventilation system.

Heidi waited until everyone else left, then heaved the cheese down from its shelf. This reward was so large she quickly tired of carrying it in her arms. Instead, she hunched over and rolled the wax wheel along the ground. When she got it home, her mother cut into it and closed her eyes, savoring the creamy richness. It may have been the most luxurious thing she had ever eaten. They traded some portions for other staples, and this invaluable food helped revive her mother. It allowed the baby inside to grow.

This had been an unimaginably trying pregnancy, but now, she was keeping food down. There could scarcely be a more perfect food than this high-fat, high-protein cheese.

That fall, the Red Cross set up makeshift neighborhood schools. The children might only have one book between eight or nine children of different ages, but the promise of canned chicken noodle soup and a piece of bread lured feral children from the streets.

When people heard that airplanes were dropping candy, adults cautioned the children to never touch anything from the sky.

A Child In Berlin

"It is a trick. The Americans dust it with phosphorus to burn your hands and eyes."[5] She never found any, but she would probably have taken her chances if she had.

The Red Cross also brought medicine and gave the children shots for typhoid and diphtheria. In addition, they treated the children for scabies brought in by the Russian soldiers. It is caused by a mite that burrows under the skin and makes a painful rash, spreading from person to person in tight quarters. So, all school children had to be painted from head to toe with a white paste.

Now surviving soldiers began returning home, and one day Richard Sauerbrey knocked on the door. He had been in a POW camp in Yugoslavia and made it back before the birth of his child.[6] Heidi's baby brother, René Sauerbrey, was born on October 30, with a middle name inadvertently given by a clerk on the birth certificate, "Sarberg," which was simply a misspelling of Sauerbrey.

He came out small and blue, but this precious little life was a testament to how ferociously every living thing will fight to carry on. He was a miracle in every way. The infant mortality rate in Berlin during that era reached as high as 90 percent, but the timing was such that he could be born

---

5   The "Candy Bomber," Gail Halverson, became famous for spreading goodwill by dropping real chocolate bars. Heidi never found any of these, and what she heard was an example of how rumors ran rampant in those days. People were rightly suspicious, especially after the Holocaust came to light.

6   Richard had been taken prisoner by Yugoslavian Partisans and received favorable treatment through a stroke of good fortune. As a young man, Richard was educated at a private school in Switzerland. It turned out that this camp's commanding officer had been one of Richard's classmates, sent for an expensive education in Switzerland. In the camp, Richard's language abilities proved useful. His old buddy, the commanding officer, granted him great freedom during his time there. One could scarcely dream up a better, safer place for him to have been during the war. He returned intact and without the traumas that would burden most survivors. And after the war, since he was not ethnically German, the Russians did not deport him to hard labor like they did to punish many former soldiers.

in a hospital, one of the first services to receive aid after the fighting ended.

Heidi was nine and a half when her baby brother was born, and she thought he looked more like a rat than a baby. She loved him anyway.

Once home, he plumped up quickly, and Richard was proud to have a son. René was a source of great joy—literal rebirth in their family. They all adored him. Heidi was tickled to be a big sister, looking after him and pushing her brother around in a white baby buggy with large wheels.

CHAPTER TWELVE

**1946 THROUGH 1949:
STARTING OVER**

DURING THE WAR, KÄTHE HAD protected her courage like a fortress under siege, but now some stress fractures showed. Pressures included nurturing a newborn, getting along with a husband she barely knew, and trying to handle a spirited preteen daughter.

When it had been only Käthe and Heidi, Käthe had forged her way on charm, resourcefulness, and sheer personal will. In the let-down period, this was a hard act to keep up. Richard and Käthe had strong personalities and fought, but soon learned to bottle it up because loud noises made little René cry, then stop breathing and go limp.

When 1945 ended, a year closed that Europe would call "Zero Hour." It takes time to rebuild a continent, and 1946 was not much better. In 1946 to 1947, Europe experienced a winter almost as harsh as 1941, and it came to be known as the "Hunger Winter."

Food and coal were in short supply everywhere. Children continued to scavenge for whatever they could find, and Heidi went out gathering bits of coal. The children would hop onto the back of Russian coal trucks and toss bits of coal onto the street behind to the children who followed. They also went gathering wood from anywhere she could find some, but many of the city's trees were gone by then.

With these coal bits, Heidi's family made little fires to dry out her brother's diapers.

Heidi also filled her time by knitting all her brothers' clothes in the method that Oma had taught her. She made his little leggings, sweaters, and hats. He was such a cute little guy. Heidi also made some of her own clothing, including a two-piece bathing suit made of flour sack yarn, which she used when she and her brother went to the pool. She was so proud of her suit until she got in the pool, and it waterlogged, stretching in embarrassing ways. She only sunbathed in it after that.

Heidi often thought of Oma in the village and longed to go back for a visit, but infrastructure had been destroyed at the end of the war. When train service did resume, everyone experienced such hardship and restrictions under Russian occupation that travel was out of reach for them.[1]

By the time Heidi turned ten in March of 1946, her brother had grown into a beautiful little boy with his mother's eyes, although he constantly suffered from ear infections and other ailments.

For whatever reason—their language abilities, or because they were not German—Russian communists befriended their little family. Soon they were issued a well-appointed apartment in Berlin Pankow, a prominent part of the Russian sector. They left Alexanderplatz and said goodbye to an entire neighborhood that would be demolished and not rebuilt—only to exist in memory after that.

Their new place was on Kavalierstrasse near Schönhausen Palace and park, and Heidi answered the phone by giving the number 480262. She enrolled in school and could finally attend regularly, falling in with a group of friends right

---

1   Heidi would never make it back to the village and would never see her beloved Oma again before Oma passed away of natural causes late in life.

away. She was the new girl, but wasn't everyone at that time? Everyone was being put back together in one way or another.

She and her friends played sports in the park, where she practiced pulling herself up on the bars and balancing her body in just about any position with the strength of her arms and abdomen. Walking to and from school, she usually picked a route with fences she could climb onto and then balance-beam walk most of the way.

On rainy days, she had a Little Ben alarm clock that she practiced taking apart and putting back together until it worked again. She got faster and faster at this—one of her favorite things to do because there were not a lot of toys around.

But she struggled academically because she had never been in one school long enough to gain a proper foundation in written German. When she looked at the words on the paper, they appeared jumbled and mixed up. She couldn't figure out why the printed page seemed so foreign to her when she so easily picked up spoken languages.

In that school, she also discovered that she had different ideas about how the world worked. Once, when she turned in an assigned paper about the oceans, she wrote, "I think human life started in the sea."

Her teacher crossed that part out with a red pencil and said, "Don't make ridiculous statements!"

She felt awash in a familiar shame that others did not think she was very bright. Privately, however, she did not change her mind and held a personal hunch about the oceans. She never remembered being taught this anywhere or hearing it; she simply thought it seemed right. That experience gave her an important lesson about school; after that, she kept thoughts like that to herself.

Käthe continued sending Heidi to church, and when Heidi and René were invited to the priest's home for lunch, she carried René a long distance. René had become a cute, chunky boy by now and was hard to lug around, but a good meal for both was too important to pass. Their little family was no longer starving, but most people were still hungry all the time, and Heidi was never sure if or how her parents were eating.

Richard was an accountant by trade who could do complicated math in his head. Käthe found work as a bartender. Heidi did not know the details of the grownups' lives, but the family was doing considerably better than before, improving all the time. Käthe would sometimes come home with items for the apartment and was fond of the beautiful furniture she acquired, including Chippendale dining room furniture from the sixteenth century.

The years from age ten through thirteen passed peacefully for Heidi and a period of three years ran together, seeming much shorter than it was. Time can play strange tricks on a person's memories. The year 1945 had been a lifetime on its own, and in the war's final push, days and weeks felt like whole years. In earlier times, Heidi had processed fleeting inputs on instinct, and images became burned in her mind with photographic clarity. She remembered everything from those days. Now that she could relax, however, Heidi's memories blurred into soft-focus generalities, except for a few episodes that were kept in her recollections.

There was some turbulence at home, however. René suffered from chronic ear infections, and by the time he was three, he was complaining of pain in his side and leg. Finally, a doctor had a theory that the ear infection had leaked down to the area surrounding his kidney, and they performed surgery. They cut into the poor little guy from one side of his body to the other, found the infection, and inserted a drainage tube so he could finally heal. He improved a great deal after that.

Heidi turned twelve in 1948, and Christmas brought the most lavish presents the children had ever received. Her mother found a steel pedal car for René that was so sturdy even Heidi could get in it. Heidi received three dresses, which her mother would have her seamstress alter for a perfect fit. One had tiny stripes with green, orange, and blue. If you stepped back, it looked orange, but you could see the fine lines up close. Another was a navy-blue wool dress with a red collar and pockets, and buttonholes in red. She also received new silk underwear. The best gift of all, one that she and her brother would cherish, was a sled made of smooth wooden planks and metal runners.

On Christmas Day, she took it to the park and tried her skill on a large hillside that bottomed out at a creek. Locals called it the "cat's back" because its shape was like a cat that had arched its back.

Heidi laid face forward and steered by shifting her body weight. Her sense of balance made her a natural at maneuvering it, so she never ended up in the creek like some children. She stayed out there from morning to dusk, only coming in for supper. It never occurred to her to feel cold until she hiked back, dragging her sled by the cord behind her. She realized then that she had been soaked through for hours.

One episode that remained in her memory was when Heidi began picking up on the unusual activities of other residents in the building in the spring of 1949. Heidi's family sublet a room in their flat to a Russian man, and when his door opened, Heidi saw that he had money lying around. She did not know how he made his living, but he spent a lot of money and flaunted it. His bold displays when others were so frugal made her wonder why. Once when Heidi was playing with other children, she saw him pass and remarked, "How does he make so much money?"

One of the children shrugged. "He's a Stasi."

Heidi asked, "What's a Stasi?"

"A spy, you idiot."

Heidi was skeptical. "He's a very nice man."

The boy shrugged. "A spy knows how to insinuate himself."

Heidi pushed back, "You're making up stories. If he's a spy, then why would he be so careless? He attracts attention."

The boy assumed an air of authority. "He waves money on purpose. He already recruited your whole building."

At this, Heidi was incredulous, "My parents aren't spies."

The boy said, "If they aren't now, they will be."

At home, Heidi asked her mother, "What's a Stasi?"

Her mother contemplated the question. "Who's asking?"

Heidi shrugged. "I don't know. Kids talk."

Her mother said, "They shouldn't—you shouldn't. Stasis work for the communist party."

Heidi asked, "Are you a communist?"

"No."

Then her mother assumed the same tone as she had during the war. She placed her hands on the girl's shoulders and looked straight into Heidi's eyes.

"Remember what I taught you. If someone asks you a question, you shrug. You know nothing. You must not gossip with your friends. This is playing with fire. Do you understand?"

A chill passed through Heidi. Her mother was hauled away the last time she had been drilled on this procedure.

Heidi began noticing the activities of everyone in the building and noticed that they were better off than people in other buildings. Heidi wondered why. Her mother was a bartender who could not make a big income. Richard did not have a steady job, instead staying home to look after the children while his wife worked. Could it be true that her building really was full of spies? Was a spy living right under their noses, in a room of their very home?

A few days later, her mother returned from work, and when Heidi looked up, her mother held out an old cigar box as though bearing a gift. "Open it."

Heidi lifted the lid to see two pure white mice peering at her with pink eyes, their noses twitching. They seemed content there, not taking the opportunity to bolt when the lid opened. Heidi was in love, and the new pets worked as her mother had intended for the day, distracting Heidi's attention. But not for long. The next day while her parents were occupied and their roommate headed out, he left his door room ajar. Heidi couldn't help her curiosity, and she crept in. His place was cluttered, and she saw a billfold of cash on his dresser and crumpled currency in random places. This man treated money like it was scratch paper.

When he returned that afternoon, he paid her mother his rent from his billfold, and Heidi overheard their conversation. He was apparently trying to persuade Käthe to do something, "You're smart, and the languages you both speak are valuable."

"You flatter us."

The man continued, "You would be rewarded."

Käthe seemed enthusiastic as she said, "How could we say no? Let me talk with Richard."

But Käthe possessed the skill of every good bartender—seeming to agree with everyone, acting interested, while postponing any action.

Heidi's stomach knotted. Had her friend been right? How had they been assigned such a desirable apartment in the first place?

A few days later, Heidi's parents closed their bedroom door to discuss something. Heidi tiptoed to the door and listened in. Their voices were too quiet to make out the conversation, but they seemed heated. She only made out one word for sure, "Summoned."

Heidi again tiptoed back to her mice and acted oblivious.

Her mother announced, "Today, we are doing some paperwork with the authorities. Gerda downstairs will watch you."

Heidi's heart was pounding, and her mouth was dry as sandpaper. She interrogated her mother. "When will you be back?"

Her mother was vague, "Oh, not long."

Heidi pressed for more. "Are you in trouble?"

Her mother brushed off the question. "No need to worry. Just something with your father's visa."

"Then you can stay, and he can go."

Her mother was firm. "We must both appear."

Her parents did not come back that night, and Gerda stayed with the children in their apartment. Heidi slept fitfully and was awakened by her old nightmare.

Her parents did not come back the next day. Heidi tried to distract herself by entertaining her brother, but she was anxious. Gerda came back to stay with the children again that night.

Heidi again tossed in bed that night, her mind racing in a loop of worry.

What if they don't return? I'm too young to become René's mother.

Eventually, sleep overtook her mind until she jolted straight upright at the sound of a key in the lock. She raced to the door, her heart pounding. She could hear her mother's voice on the other side. When the door opened, she flung herself into her mother's arms before they stepped across the threshold.

Käthe embraced Heidi and kissed the top of her head hard. "My Heidilein."

Heidi held this stance for a long time, then pushed away. Now she was angry. "Why didn't you call?"

Her mother's lipstick looked fresh, as though she had thought to put it on just before opening the door, but her hair was disheveled, and she wore heavy circles under her eyes. She looked like she had aged years but ignored the girl's rage and smiled brightly.

"You act like we weren't coming back."

Her mother went to bed and slept for almost twenty-four hours. The following day after their roommate left, Heidi noticed her mother arranging clothing with items selected for each family member. She retrieved her sewing box, and Heidi thought she intended to mend their clothes, except that she had brought out their favorite things, articles that did not need repair.

Then, she spied her mother sewing jewelry and other valuables into the linings. When Heidi asked what she was doing, her mother replied. "We have some business to take care of in the west, and one can never be too careful when traveling."

Heidi tried asking more questions, but Käthe shot her a look that meant, *I don't have patience for you right now.*

Käthe worked on this activity over the next few days.

Then she announced to Heidi, "I am ready to tell you. Tomorrow, we're going to visit Lizzie in Stuttgart!"

In earlier years, they would often take the U-Bahn or S-Bahn across the whole city, and she had been to Poland and the Czech countryside. But now, going to Stuttgart meant leaving Russian territory and venturing into the American sector. This was big news. Immediately after the war ended, Berliners traveled freely, but the Russians began cracking down. Now, people were only granted permission to travel beyond the border if they returned before midnight.

They would depart by train early in the morning since they had to return the same day.

That evening, Käthe had instructions for Heidi.

"Our papers were almost impossible to get, and you didn't need them before you turned thirteen. So, if anyone asks your age, you are twelve years old."

Käthe drilled Heidi until she was convinced by the girl's answers. "How old are you? Twelve. What's your birthday? March 12, 1937. What year were you born? 1937. What is your grade in school? Again!"

The drill triggered Heidi's anxiety, but they practiced until she could respond without thinking. In the morning, as Heidi dressed, her mother instructed her to wear two sets of underwear and two pairs of socks. While getting ready, her mother asked, "What year were you born?" Heidi responded without hesitating, "1937."

Just as they were about to lock the apartment, Käthe paused like she was trying to remember something.

Then she said, "Heidi, why don't you bring your mice?"

Heidi delighted at having them accompany her on their grand adventure, and she shuttled them into the cigar box.

On the train, their little family sat across the aisle from an older couple who made conversation.

When Heidi took out her mice to play, the lady inquired about the pets. Heidi showed them off, and the lady admired how cute and tame they were. Want to hold them? Heidi was just about to hand the box over when a pair of soldiers—one Russian and one German—came down the aisle checking papers.

They stopped in front of them, and the German one asked Heidi, "What's in the box?"

Heidi grinned and opened the box for him to see, "My pets!" It didn't cross her mind to worry that they might be confiscated.

When the soldier saw them, he said, "I had pet mice as a boy!" He smiled and became mesmerized by their soft white fur and little squeaks.

After a moment, he remembered his job and asked for their papers but only gave them a cursory glance, apparently still distracted by the mice. He moved on without further questions. Either he didn't notice that there were no papers for Heidi or assumed she was still a child.

When it was time for a snack, Heidi put her pets back into their box and stowed them in the compartment above the other couple's seats. At the next stop, the polite couple left the train.

Before the train pulled away from the station, Heidi's family turned with a jolt at pounding on the window. The woman, out of breath, had come back to the train in a panic. In her hands, she cupped one of Heidi's mice. It had crawled from its box and into the woman's hat. The husband noticed it there, and the woman shrieked. Rather than being angry or turning the mouse loose, she returned it to Heidi.

"Now, don't let this one out of your sight. You would be heartbroken to lose your pets."

Heidi peered out the window as the morning brightened. Heidi noticed that the further into the west they got, the towns got cleaner, and people wore more vibrant clothes.

In the American sector, people were smiling, and buildings were painted. People's gardens flourished, and children carried toys. Of course, it was still Germany, but a different world.

They stepped off the train into beautiful Stuttgart with its red tile roofs and hills of vineyards.

Heidi looked around for Lizzie. "Where is she?"

Her mother shushed her and then shuttled them away from the station before saying, "We are not going to see

Lizzie today. And we are not going back to Kavalierstrasse tonight. By the grace of God, not ever."

Instead, they went straightaway to file for political asylum.

They waited in a room overflowing with weary people. Babies wailed, and parents tried to entertain restless children. Then, finally, their names were called back for a short interview. Heidi's eyes widened to hear her mother tell the whole story. Since both she and Richard spoke multiple languages, unbeknownst to them, they had been assigned to live in a building seeded with communist spies. When they refused to join the cause, they were called in for questioning and given an ultimatum. They had to flee or face dire consequences for not playing along.

A man stamped their papers, and they were directed to a bus that deposited them at a Red Cross refugee camp.

Before retiring for the night, they received a tour: wash facilities consisted of one long trough with faucets and meager meal rations served mess style. This was not the adventure Heidi had imagined when she wore her favorite dress that morning.

How had she not seen this coming when her mother started sewing jewelry into their clothes?

In a single day, they had gone from the dreary east to the vibrant west, but they had also traded a posh apartment for wooden barracks. Instead of comfortable beds, they had straw mattresses.

Now Heidi realized that this dress, another one under it, her coat, two pairs of underwear, and her pet mice were all that she possessed in the world. Her sled and ice skates would go to another child.

They were back to where they started after the war, bombed out.

Still, she had to acknowledge that her mother had not been taken away. As long as they were together, they would be okay. They had started with nothing before, and they could do it again.

Käthe also said, "In Stuttgart, we can say what we want about the Russians. They no longer control our lives. And you are now free to become anything you want. We left our past, so you can have a future."

Throughout the camp, Heidi heard languages from all over Eastern Europe. She could communicate with about anyone with the Polish, Czech, and Russian she already understood.

Refugees had converged there from many countries, biding their time until they could be processed and assigned housing. Some had been there quite a while because of the sheer number of asylum seekers and refugees who refused repatriation following the war.

They soon learned that illnesses were rampant there, and the transient nature of that camp made them uneasy.

Käthe immediately went to work looking for a better situation, figuring out what it would take to get there. Before long, she had orchestrated a transfer from that temporary camp into a former Nazi Army barracks outside Stuttgart. It was a brick building, several stories tall with showers, kitchens for feeding masses, and private family rooms. It was a much better place to stay until their paperwork came through.

The facilities were built for permanence and cleanliness, and each refugee received a weekly card that was stamped at mealtimes. The food was hot and provided by the Red Cross, often including cabbage, potato soup, and corn with everything: cornbread, corn mush, creamed corn, and canned corn. Although Heidi was glad for something to eat, she could never stomach canned corn afterward.

Their situation had improved by a degree, but this was still a dreary place, and people lay around all day without purpose or hope. It also smelled foul, and nobody wanted to use the filthy showers.

Käthe wasn't having it.

She kept their room spotless, washed their underclothes each night with a bar of soap, then hung them up to dry.

She told Heidi, "We might be poor, but there is no excuse to be dirty. You can always find a bar of soap and some water. *Always.*"

Before they took a shower, Käthe cleaned it herself.

Heidi was still wetting the bed, so each morning, she had to take her straw mat outside, remove all the straw, wash the covering, rinse the straw, and let it all dry in the sun. Heidi did not mind the task itself, but she felt deep embarrassment because everyone would know that she was still wetting the bed at age thirteen. Again, she felt the judging eyes of people who had nothing better to do than gossip.

Meanwhile, they made contact with Richard's sister Elsa in Switzerland, and she began sending them care packages of coffee and chocolate—luxuries you couldn't usually get in a refugee camp. Käthe stockpiled these until she had an impressive cache.

Käthe hatched a plan. She could use these items to coax the man in charge into going along with her. She wanted to get everyone moving into productive activity each day. The way to motivate people was with food; the man in charge controlled the meal tickets.

They packed a box of desirable items and brought them to the man in charge.

She said, "Okay, we've got to make a deal. I will give you all this, but I want you to let me take care of these people. You give me the fresh meal tickets each week, and I will assign everyone to clean this place. When they get their work done, they get their tickets."

He agreed, and she organized a group of leaders who helped her assign jobs to everyone.

"You clean the toilets, and you clean the showers. Then, when you finish, you get paid."

Next, they assigned people to clean the top floor. "There are tables and chairs up there. Sweep the floor and set up desks. We are going to start school." She went around asking, "Has anybody ever taught anything? Do we have any books?" Everyone had something meaningful to do.

Soon the place looked and smelled presentable. People began bathing, and a spark returned to their eyes when they had accomplished something. Her initiative made all the difference in that place.

Heidi was intrigued by the people there who had come from Eastern Europe, many in wagons loaded with their household goods. Heidi was especially taken with the Czechs, who gathered around fires outside and sang traditional songs. She thought of her father, the woodworker.

Käthe put her bartering skills to work and acquired a beautiful sewing table at least two hundred years old. It added an element of warmth and hominess to their little room.

It was summer, and the children dug a hole under the barbed wire fence and stole green apples from the orchard just beyond. Then, they made fires and roasted them so they would not get diarrhea. This treat brought Heidi back to the forest with her Oma.

It took months for the authorities to check their background and process them out of the camp. Heidi's family had been on a list to move into housing, but so many buildings were bombed that options were scarce. Any family with an extra room had to take on displaced people, and these families were not generally happy about sharing their homes with strangers. Who would be?

Finally, they were assigned to live with a couple who had extra rooms. They processed out of the camp and received forty marks per head to get on their feet.

In this couple's apartment, Käthe, Richard, René, and Heidi crammed into a single bedroom with Richard and René sleeping on one bed and Heidi and her mother on another. They shared the kitchen.

Heidi's family did their best to be quiet, clean up after themselves and not impose. The couple also tried to be cordial, but it was a strain. The man had returned from the war injured, and they argued a lot, with big explosive outbursts. The stress of having strangers live under their roof only added to the tension. The whole situation was a tinderbox.

Within a few weeks, Käthe arranged for them to move in with Lizzie, who lived alone in an attic apartment. It was smaller than the couple's apartment, but it felt more expansive without all the tension.

Lizzie kept her room while Käthe, Richard, and René slept in the other. Heidi slept on a laundry bag in the kitchen for lack of a real bed. They shared the kitchenette, and the bathroom consisted of a toilet and sink but no shower. This meant they took sponge baths most of the time.

Heidi's mother said of these sponge baths, "First, you set your pan on the counter and wash down as far as possible. Then, you put the pan on the floor and wash up as far as possible. *Then you wash possible.*" She delivered the joke with a mischievous glint in her eye.

They resumed their Berlin routine of going to a public bathhouse once a week to get fully clean.

They had no steady jobs yet, and so they were grateful for every kindness given and every necessity they had. For example, a baker in the neighborhood who learned they

A Child In Berlin

were refugees set aside loaves of bread they could pick up for free. He sent them off without a fuss.

Heidi often took René to a park with playground equipment, including ropes on a pole, where four or five children had to work together to get it moving and in balance. They sometimes climbed up to the planetarium, too.

One day, Heidi was out with René after a rainstorm, and two well-dressed men were about to sit down on a bench, deep in conversation.

Heidi interrupted them. "Sir, don't sit there. It's wet, and you will ruin your beautiful suit."

The man was impressed. "Thank you. Where are you from?"

Heidi told them they lived nearby. The man said, "That is a Berlin accent, no?"

"Yes, we escaped the east, first to a refugee camp and now here."

The man asked, "Were you there during the war?"

Heidi nodded.

Then he asked a curious question.

"Do you like the movies?"

"I *love* the movies."

He motioned the children to come to the theater across the street. Inside, he asked for the manager, who seemed to know him.

"Any time these children come to the movies, you let them in and charge me."

It turned out that the man owned the theater. Heidi and René went to a lot of movies after that, often telling her mother they were going to the park instead. She thought children should be outside playing or else studying, not filling their heads with frivolous nonsense onscreen.

One time Heidi instructed René, "Don't tell Mútti we went to the movies."

So, when they got home, he marched up to her and proudly announced, "We didn't go to the movies."

Heidi was in trouble for getting her little brother to lie.

And so, that is how it was after the war for Germany's children. Heidi slid back into childhood, and she transitioned into adolescence in Stuttgart. The children were more resilient than adults, growing up beyond their years, and bearing witness to events no child should have to see. She wondered, *Why am I here when so many others are not? Why me and not Uschi?*

The grownups asked themselves the same questions. They wore their grief and their shame as a verdict. They carried on for their children. They carried on as though living were a duty that only the survivors could fulfill. Carrying on was a penance borne by the living. It was not borne by the ones who died without a choice, nor was it borne by the ones who chose to die. In the rebuilding years, who would have traded places with whom, the living or the dead? It was best not to dwell on those questions. They were a conquered people, and it would take another generation before they could begin feeling pride in their country again.

Heidi would never forget hunger or the feeling of being so cold her whole body felt numb. But by the time they settled in Stuttgart, those deprivations began to feel like the kind of memory a person has of winter from the vantage point of a summer picnic. One certainly remembers that the park lay blanketed in snow six months earlier and that the trees had no leaves, but it seems impossible to be the same park. It seems like someone else's life.

She was beginning to understand what her mother had meant when she would say, "By the time you are married, you will forget these troubles." But she would always remember the events of the war with sharp clarity, sometimes she wanted to recall, and sometimes she had no choice. The smell of burning garbage or a decaying animal in the forest would stop her cold, freezing her body until she could collect herself. That reaction would never leave her, even as an old woman. She would also suffer from feelings of abandonment throughout her life, especially when loved ones died.

In Stuttgart, Heidi was on the cusp of adolescence without realizing it. Not long after moving there, she got her first period and about the same time, her bed-wetting stopped altogether. In the coming years, she would make new friends, experience her first crush, and she got to spend a glorious summer in Geneva, Switzerland with Richard's family. This was her new stepfamily. Richard's sister collected a wardrobe of beautiful clothes so Heidi could enjoy herself in style. She spent that summer in a home that was so well-to-do she could hardly believe how carefree they lived. That summer would be one of the most glorious times of her whole childhood. They hiked in the Alps, they rode bikes, and Heidi learned French.

Under American occupation, Stuttgart rebuilt quickly. There were American soldiers everywhere and whenever they passed by on the street, Heidi would catch a waft of Old Spice cologne, a smell she began to associate with confidence and possibility. The soldiers were cheerful and polite, with broad smiles and generosity toward children. That is how she was given her first Baby Ruth candy bar, which she shared with her little brother. She thought it was nearly the best thing she had ever eaten.

Heidi made friends with a girl whose family in America sent the most wonderful toys. Around this time, she was introduced to America House, a place like a YMCA where teens could gather, play games, and experience American culture. She thought, "Any country that produces such wonderful food, toys, and people is where I want to go."

Her relationship with her mother and Richard became further strained through her teen years, and as she branched in her own direction, Heidi's daydreams about America became a call. How could she not hear it? She was surrounded by American culture, a stark contrast to so many bleak memories of Germany.

As her path diverged from childhood and her family of origin, so too would her feelings toward Germany. She had always felt more at home in the countryside with her Oma than in the city. The war stole Oma from her, and that period of her life was punctuated with bleakness, uncertainty, abandonment, and want. There was little German pride by anyone in those years, so she naturally turned toward a new beginning.

If the world had been different, Heidi might have spent the rest of her life visiting Oma by train and continuing her apprenticeship in the old ways, while simultaneously learning the new in Stuttgart. But that was not to be. The village became part of Poland again, which belonged to Russia. Not long after Heidi's family escaped, Russia wised up to the talent drain. Anybody with a little wherewithal or an independent streak like Käthe got out early. Those who waited became walled in.

In the ensuing years, Käthe would visit her relatives on occasion by crossing the border at the wall in Berlin. She'd meet with them at the Hotel International near Checkpoint Charlie on the border, bringing suitcases full of clothes and other items they could no longer get. She would press into their hands as much money as she could spare. There were very few restrictions on bringing gifts to relatives behind the wall; Russia only clamped down on anything or anyone *going out*.

In those visits, relatives always watched their words, looking over their shoulders, and scanning for two-way mirrors or listening devices. They took it as a given that they were being spied on. That was just part of life behind the wall.

Heidi only accompanied her mother to the wall on one of those visits, but she never made it back to the village and never got to see her Oma again. The year she had spent in late 1943 through early 1944 with Tante Hedel, her great aunt, and Oma before the war ended was the last time.

She couldn't have known then that it would be the last, but by mid-1944, as Germany collapsed, nobody felt a guarantee of anything. Going back to Berlin into the fight was one of the riskiest decisions of Käthe's life. Heidi never knew for sure what compelled her to go into the fray while others were leaving, other than she said she was needed, and she had a burning feeling that it was what she felt she needed to do. She must have also believed that Berlin would be taken by the west first, not by Russia. That belief may have fueled her desire to get as far west as possible, and certainly to take Heidi with her so they would not be separated.

Toward the end, American units often encountered little resistance in villages when they arrived. Käthe almost made it, but the fall took far longer than many expected and Alexanderplatz went to the Russian side.

Käthe's heroic will to steer her own fate and flee to the west was a testament to her spirit, a quality that Heidi inherited. One can only imagine Oma's agony watching her daughter and Heidi—the apple of her eye—getting on a train from the countryside to Berlin. They all knew what was coming, and there was nothing Oma could do.

Then US Army General Dwight Eisenhower's decision to leave Berlin to Russia was a controversial one that he would have to defend. He argued Berlin would have been a vanity target for America, costing many American lives for little strategic advantage. The war was already won by then, and Russia wanted Berlin as a trophy. Thus, Russia spent its soldiers' lives only to have the city divided anyway. America got its portion without the cost to its own people. The rest of the price was paid by the women and children of that city who were virtually undefended when hordes of vengeance-hungry soldiers were given a free pass. Heidi was lucky to have been young enough—looking even younger due to malnourishment—that she escaped that ordeal without the trauma of rape. Käthe used her wits and resources to survive with her own dignity intact, but Heidi never knew of any hidden burdens she might have borne without speaking of them. The parts of Käthe's story that Heidi did know are told here.

What Heidi saw for herself was that after the war, her mother continued to be the fun-loving person that others wanted to be around. That would never change. But Käthe did have emotional scars, and her resilience suffered, especially during Heidi's teenage years as Heidi became more headstrong. Käthe's dreams had been taken from her during the war years. She would forever hold a silent grief for what might have been, and for the people who didn't make it.

Heidi would always clash with Richard.

There were some bright spots for Käthe. Lizzie would remain a dear friend for life, and Wolfgang grew to maturity and ultimately moved to South America. Käthe stayed married to Richard until their deaths.

As Heidi's own independence blossomed, Käthe and Richard adored René and their energy went into giving him the kind of stable life that every child deserves. Richard lived for that boy.

Heidi and René would remain in touch, but their early experiences were so vastly different they would never entirely understand each other. Käthe lived until old age and passed away from cancer while living outside Stuttgart.

But before all that, there is one final scene with Heidi's family, which serves as a transition moment that brings the war years to rest.

■ ■ ■

In Stuttgart, Käthe found work in a bar where she served drinks, sang, and played the accordion. The family began to afford their own necessities. By Christmas of 1949, they had saved for a Christmas tree, and they had enough for a little celebration.

Midmorning on Christmas Eve, Käthe asked Heidi, "Would you like to go to Christmas Market?"

Heidi's eyes widened as Käthe handed money to Richard.

"Dad will take you."

Käthe helped René tug on his winter clothes in a rush. She needed every minute to cook Christmas dinner in a shared kitchen, then to get it ready to serve in a space that was their bedroom, living room, and dining room in one.

"Out! Out!" She was half-cross, half-smiling as she swatted at them with a spatula.

When Richard, Heidi, and René got off the bus, the air smelled of sweet roasted almonds, juicy bratwurst sizzling over open flames, and ginger cookies. Festival music played, and they could see a Ferris wheel high above. They took their time between activities to stretch the day: eating lunch, playing games to knock over milk bottles with a ball, and riding the Ferris wheel *twice*. They rode every ride, snacked on almonds, and Richard sipped on *glühwein*. Then, when the drooping sun withdrew its warmth, they headed home. It had been a joyous day.

When they opened the apartment door, Heidi drew in the familiar smells of Christmas dinner and *Tannenbaum*, but the apartment was dark and deathly still. Richard reached for the light switch, but it did not turn on. Lizzie had left to be with family, and Heidi's heart froze with old waves of panic.

Where was her mother? Was something wrong? Had she been taken away?

A dozen fears raced through her mind in the time it took to see a crack of light coming from their bedroom. Then, finally, they opened the door to their room, and Heidi's body relaxed.

She spotted a radiant Käthe next to the table, her face peacefully illuminated by candlelight. Her hair was done, and she wore lipstick and her best dress. She looked as though she had been resting all afternoon, but the evidence of her hard work lay everywhere.

Within arm's length of the table, the tree's tinsel glittered. Heidi's mother started the music box playing as they peeled off coats and scarves. She had set their table, and then Käthe revealed her trick.

"I unscrewed the bulbs to surprise you with the effect. Without bright lights, I see that we have everything we need: a roasted goose, a cozy room, and we have each other."

While Richard and René washed up, Heidi helped her mother in the kitchen. They plated the meal, then carried each one into their room.

Heidi savored her food, thinking it had never tasted as good as this—not even at Oma's house. After clearing the dishes, Richard led them in lighting the tree while Käthe softly played her zither. The twinkling lights and intimate space kept their voices at a whisper—their own silent night, holy night. When the candles burned themselves out, the children opened presents. The gifts were few, but they had enough. In that moment, it was enough of everything. They were going to be okay.

It was the last important event of the decade for Heidi and her family, a decade that began with Hitler invading Poland when Heidi was just three years old in Berlin.

Now, the world was ready to move into the 1950s, an era of intense rebuilding in Europe and prosperity in America. Heidi would enter womanhood, showered with many gifts the world had to offer. Every joy would be sweeter for surviving the bitter.

Her dimpled smile, good manners, and fearless nature had served her well in hard times and would serve her for what lay ahead.

EPILOGUE

THE REST OF HEIDI'S LIFE is fascinating, colorful, and worthy of another book. With that in mind, here are a few highlights.

She got pregnant by an American soldier, Clarence Park, who returned to Germany and married her. It took some time for her visa to come through, but she and their baby Andy came to Provo, Utah in 1956 when she was twenty. She learned English and had another baby named Rhonda Park. Clarence got a job as a draftsman and the couple lived in Brigham City, Utah until they divorced. After that, she moved to Ogden. While working at the Combo Club on Washington Boulevard, she met John Posnien, whose father was a German immigrant. John had grown up in Ogden above Harrison Boulevard, and at his father's passing, he took over the family business, Ogden Optical.

She and John dated for several years and married in 1962. When John's mother suffered a terrible stroke, Heidi and John moved in to take care of her at the family's second home in Huntsville. The Ogden house was sold. John and Heidi ultimately purchased the Huntsville farm from her, where Heidi still lives today. Heidi and John often sang duets together in harmony and hosted lively parties. Friends came up to the lake for barbecues in the summer and skiing in the winter. Heidi's love stories are for another day.

On the farm, Heidi enjoyed what she loved most in the world: freedom, motherhood, and a menagerie of animals.

They bred horses, peacocks, and even a bobcat. He would come indoors, leap on top of the refrigerator in a single bound, and then play catch with Heidi. She'd toss a squishy ball, and the bobcat would bat it back.

Heidi and John mingled with Ogden's society and business community, just as easily as with their hippie friends and small-town neighbors. Their friends were a colorful cast of characters.

Heidi began modeling for Utah Tailoring Mills and did so for over twenty years, appearing in ads and traveling to their fashion shows. She was tall and stunning, having a natural sense of stage presence and grace inherited from her mother. Some neighbors dubbed Heidi and John "The Hollywood couple," because they once hosted a movie crew on their property and because they had that type of glamour when they dressed up.

Käthe visited Huntsville and enjoyed seeing her grandchildren, but she could never understand why Heidi would choose to live in the country. René and his wife also visited, as well as some of the other extended family. Heidi and her daughter Rhonda went back to Germany a few times, but Heidi never made it back to Oma's village. Heidi got her US citizenship and was fond of speaking to others about what America means to her, having known the contrast both in Nazi Germany and while living under communism.

She and John purchased the Shooting Star Saloon in Huntsville, which is the oldest continuously operating bar in Utah today. It was a sleepy bar at the time they took it over, but the pair put it on the map, playing up the western décor, having a lively atmosphere, and serving delicious burgers. Heidi kept an immaculately clean establishment, and they made it such a fun place that it became a destination for out-of-towners.

As of the release of this book in late 2024, Heidi is eighty-eight with a sharp mind and quick sense of humor. She still cares for her property. Her spunky French bulldog is named Lizzie. Her home feels like a respite, nestled in a rural community.

She has outlived nearly everyone in her family, including her children. Andy was tragically killed in an automobile accident in 1985 at the age of thirty, leaving behind a wife and two young children. Rhonda suffered from type 1 diabetes and only had one child, a baby who lived just a few precious hours. Rhonda died from cancer and complications related to juvenile diabetes in 2009 at the age of fifty-two. Heidi's husband John passed away in 2014.

Heidi has a fond relationship with two grown grandchildren from her son Andy: Andrea lives in Colorado with her partner Casandra, and Andre lives in Japan following his career in the US Marine Corps.

The sense of independence Heidi had as a child, and the fact that she is peaceful on her own, has served her well at this phase of life. She often walks her dog after dark, even in the winter with her feet crunching in the snow. It reminds her of being in the village with her Oma as a child. Heidi still looks up at the moon, and she does not feel alone.

BIBLIOGRAPHY

Abandoned Playgrounds (website no longer available). Accessed September 14, 2023. .

"Adolf Hitler and Vegetarianism." Wikipedia. Accessed September 14, 2023. https://en.wikipedia.org/w/index.php?title=Adolf_Hitler_and_vegetarianism&oldid=1172198366.

"Alt-Hohenschönhausen." Wikipedia. Accessed September 12, 2023. https://en.wikipedia.org/wiki/Alt-Hohensch%C3%B6nhausen.

Ambrose, Stephen E. *Eisenhower and Berlin, 1945: The Decision to Halt at the Elbe.* New York: W.W. Norton, 2000.

"Battle of Berlin." Wikipedia. Accessed September 14, 2023. https://en.wikipedia.org/wiki/Battle_of_Berlin.

Beevor, Antony. "'The Russian Soldiers Raped Every German Female from Eight to 80.'" *The Guardian*, May 1, 2002. https://www.theguardian.com/books/2002/may/01/news.features11.

"Berlin Alexanderplatz Station." Wikipedia. Accessed September 14, 2023. https://en.wikipedia.org/w/index.php?title=Berlin_Alexanderplatz_station&oldid=1158729676.

Berlin: Allied Intelligence Map of Key Buildings. London: Photolithographed by War Office, 1945.

"Berlin State Opera House, Berlin - Germany." Meet Me at the Opera. Accessed September 14, 2023. https://meetmeattheopera.com/opera-houses/berlin-opera-house/.

"Berolina." Wikipedia. Accessed September 14, 2023. https://en.wikipedia.org/w/index.php?title=Berolina&oldid=1089044333.

Beskidzki, Kris. "Bytom - Szyb Zachodni KWK Miechowice." Krisowe Szlaki i Bezdroża. February 1, 2013. http://szlakiibezdroza.blogspot.com/2013/02/bytom-szyb-zachodni-kwk-miechowice.html.

Dugard, Martin. *Taking Berlin: The Bloody Race to Defeat the Third Reich.* US.: Dutton Caliber, 2023.

"Eva von Tiele-Winckler." Wikipedia. Accessed September 12, 2023. https://de.wikipedia.org/wiki/Eva_von_Tiele-Winckler.

"Gedenkstätte Und Museum Sachsenhausen (Sachsenhausen Memorial and Museum)." Sachsenhausen Memorial and Museum. Accessed June 1, 2023. https://www.sachsenhausen-sbg.de/en/.

Google Maps. https://www.google.com/maps/. Special thanks to Google Maps' street view and directions to substantiate Heidi's memory of locations and distances, and especially for giving us a glimpse into Oma's village as it is today. What an amazing technology we have now that we could see the cathedral and walk the streets without being in a place Heidi has not seen since the 1940s.

"History and Situation in Poland." Evangelical Church of the Augsburg Confession in Poland. Accessed June 11, 2023. https://en.luteranie.pl/history/.

Kopleck, Maik. *Berlin 1933–1945: Past Finder – Traces of German History: A Guidebook*, English edition. Berlin: Links, 2008.

"Magda Goebbels." Wikipedia. Accessed September 14, 2023. https://en.wikipedia.org/w/index.php?title=Magda_Goebbels&oldid=1174274191.

Matzen, Christina. "Women's Prisons and the Politics of Punishment in Nazi and Postwar Germany." Thesis, Department of History, University of Toronto, 2022.

McCormack, David. *The Berlin 1945 Battlefield Guide: Part 1 – The Battle of the Oder-Neisse*. Oxford, UK: Fonthill Media, 2017.

McCormack, David. *The Berlin 1945 Battlefield Guide: Part 2 – The Battle of Berlin*. Oxford, UK: Fonthill Media, 2017.

"Miechowice." Second Wiki. Accessed September 14, 2023. https://second.wiki/wiki/miechowice.

Moorhouse, Roger. *Berlin at War*. New York: Basic Books, 2012. Special thanks are in order for this wonderful book, which I listened to and read via Audible, a hard copy, and a Kindle version so I could search. The research was impeccable, substantiating many details from Heidi's memory and providing others to supplement her memory. For example, many of the news clippings and jokes that made the rounds came from this book.

Nasze Miechowice. "Miechowice Wczoraj i Dziś," YouTube, October 20, 2014. Video, 6:44. https://www.youtube.com/watch?app=desktop&v=m49aCW-33x0.

Robinson, Matt. "The Battle of Berlin 1945: A Day-by-Day Account." Berlin Experiences, April 14, 2020. https://www.berlinexperiences.com/the-battle-of-berlin-1945-a-day-by-day-account/. I want to give a special thanks to the author of this article because their day-by-day account was immensely helpful with the details needed to piece together the timeline and locations of the events of April and May 1945.

Ryan, Cornelius. *The Last Battle: The Classic History of the Battle of Berlin.* New York, NY: Simon & Schuster, 1966. We wish to extend gratitude for the excellent research in this book and its descriptions of behind-the-scene moments with Hitler and his top generals.

Ullrich, Volker. *Eight Days in May: The Final Collapse of the Third Reich.* New York, NY: W.W. Norton & Company, 2023. Originally published in German as *Acht Tage im Mai: Die Letzte Woche des Dritten Reiches.*

Vinciguerra, Thomas. "Duty Calls: Dinner with the Führer." *The New York Times*, March 7, 2009.

REVIEW INQUIRY

Hi, it's Rhonda Lauritzen here. I hope you found the story of Heidi and her mother inspiring. It was a labor of love and a joy to write.

I have a favor to ask you.

Would you consider giving it a rating wherever you bought the book? Stores are more likely to promote a book when they feel good about its content, and reader reviews are a great barometer of a book's quality.

So please go to the website wherever you bought it, search for the title, and leave a review. I even encourage you to include a picture of you holding it, which increases the likelihood that your review will be accepted.

Many thanks in advance,
Rhonda Lauritzen

ABOUT THE AUTHOR

Rhonda Lauritzen has been a full-time professional author since 2017 at Evalogue.Life and teaches weekly classes on how to write compelling true-life stories including memoir, autobiography, and family history at https://learning.evalogue.life.

She regularly speaks at international conferences like RootsTech, is a podcast guest, and does keynotes at family history events.

Rhonda was selected as the outstanding graduate in her major at Weber State University. She then earned an MBA in marketing and entrepreneurship from the University of Utah. She also served a three-year stint as CEO of her family's business, Mineral Resources International. When she decided to venture out on her own, she became the marketing director and then a vice president for the Ogden-Weber Technical College for more than a decade.

Rhonda lives with her husband and daughter in rural Weber County, Utah (outside Ogden) where they have chickens, honeybees, and a large garden. They often enjoy camping and other outdoor activities.

Made in United States
North Haven, CT
08 February 2025